PRAYING
THE
ANGELUS

"Jean-François Millet's famous painting *The Angelus* captures workers of long ago stopping to pray in the field. In a modern context, Jared Dees leads busy people to appreciate this biblically-rooted devotion and, through guided meditations, makes this ancient prayer of the Church come beautifully alive once again."

Most Rev. Joseph E. Kurtz
Archbishop of Louisville
Former president of the United States Conference
of Catholic Bishops

"*Praying the Angelus* is a necessary read for those seeking to develop an interior life based around the discipline of prayer. With the gift of a teacher, Dees treats the Angelus not simply as an ancient practice but as a school of prayer for the modern person."

Timothy O'Malley
Director of the Notre Dame Center for Liturgy

"Excellent, excellent work by Jared Dees. The best explanation of the Angelus I've seen yet, expanded with background, solid Catholic teachings, and personal anecdotes that bring this traditional Catholic devotion to life. This really is a keeper!"

Marge Fenelon
Author of *Our Lady, Undoer of Knots*

FIND JOY, PEACE, AND
PURPOSE IN EVERYDAY LIFE

PRAYING
THE
ANGELUS

JARED DEES

AVE MARIA PRESS AVE Notre Dame, Indiana

© 2017 by Jared Dees

Founded in 1865, Ave Maria Press is a ministry of the United States Province of Holy Cross.

www.avemariapress.com

Paperback: ISBN-13 978-1-59471-673-7

E-book: ISBN-13 978-1-59471-674-4

Cover image © iStockphoto.

Cover and text design by Andy Wagoner.

Printed and bound in the United States of America.

Library of Congress Cataloging-in-Publication Data is available.

Contents

Preface

Mary thought she had her life all figured out. She was engaged to a great man. They had a home in Nazareth, where people knew and respected them. Their future together was bright. Then, suddenly, everything changed: an angel appeared to Mary and told her that God had something totally different in mind for her. Mary had a difficult choice to make. Should she stick to her own plans and dreams or choose to trust in and assent to God's will for her? It is a choice we must all make at various points in our lives.

Like Mary, for many years I thought I had my life as a Catholic disciple of Christ all worked out. I had a love for scripture and the Eucharist, but the rest of our Catholic traditions seemed a bit much for me. Though I'm not a convert, I did spend a lot of time as a child with my Mississippi-born grandparents in Baptist churches. Years later, after an encounter with Christ in the Eucharist as a teenager, I fully embraced my Catholic faith and became obsessed with learning everything I could about Catholic teachings. I was all in—except that it took me a very long time to fully embrace the Catholic devotional life.

As a faithful Catholic, I was aware of and wasn't opposed to Mary, the Rosary, or other Catholic devotions, but I tended to have a less structured, more Protestant sort of prayer life and never felt the need to practice them. In college and early adulthood, I would try out new devotions and then stop. I gave the excuse most others do when dipping into new prayer practices: I just didn't get anything out of them. They seemed nice, but outside of Lent and Advent, I simply reverted to praying whenever I felt like it. That spontaneous kind of prayer made me feel good, whereas I felt that daily devotional practices took up too much time and didn't inspired me enough to stick with them.

But God had something totally different in mind for me. Today, my days are structured around a series of Catholic devotional practices. I wake up each morning and read the daily Mass readings, practicing an abbreviated form of lectio divina. I pray one decade of the Rosary with my daughters on the way to school and the remaining four on my way to work. I end my workday with an abbreviated form of the Ignatian examen. But most important, at six o'clock in the morning, noon, and six in the evening, I pray the Angelus.

Praying the Angelus has become for me a richly transformative devotion, the cornerstone habit upon which my entire personal prayer life is built. My discovering it was the first falling domino that set off a series of explorations into the beauty of Catholic devotional practices. But just ten years ago, I had never even heard of the Angelus.

As a theology teacher in a Catholic high school and a master's degree student at the University of Notre Dame, I was happy to be in Rome for the first time on a vacation with my soon-to-be wife's family and couldn't wait to see all the famous statues, buildings, and places I had read about and studied over the years. I had worked hard at understanding Catholicism and thought I knew it all.

Directly after a long, overnight flight, the family and I attended Sunday Mass at St. Peter's, sleepy though we were. Opening the doors of the basilica after Mass, we looked out into the large square just a few minutes before noon on a beautiful Sunday morning. I was surprised to see the large number of people waiting there to see the pope. Just an hour or so earlier, the square had been almost completely empty.

We wandered into the crowd and found a spot with a good view of the window where the Holy Father would soon appear. To cheers and applause, Pope Benedict XVI waved from the window and greeted the crowd. He gave an address in Italian and finished by greeting us in various other languages, including English. Then he led us in a Latin prayer that I had never heard before.

Some of the people around me joined in for the responses (they must have been there before, I thought). Embarrassed, I mumbled my way through it, hoping no one in my group would notice that this Catholic high school theology teacher had no idea what to say. What a blow to my pride! I hoped even more that no one would ask me what we were doing because, frankly, I didn't know that we were praying the Angelus or even what the Angelus was. If someone had asked, I probably would have said it was just a fancy way of naming a pope's Sunday address to the public. I knew nothing about the rich history of the prayer or the powerful impact this devotion could have on a person. I had no inkling of the impact it would have on me years later.

I never asked anyone about those Latin words. I just kind of accepted that it was something Catholics do—something ancient and important, like Stations of the Cross, the Rosary, novenas, or Eucharistic adoration. No one told me about the Angelus. No one invited me to pray it with them, and it never occurred to me to start praying it myself. I simply tucked my experience with the prayer away as part of the fond memories of my trip to Rome. I might never have prayed the Angelus again if it hadn't been for a newly ordained priest named Fr. Terry.

Once each month the parish religious education program in which I now teach schedules "Catechesis with Father." We catechists get a break from teaching and bring our classes together to be taught by our pastor or associate pastor. One November evening five years after my visit to Rome, I escorted my third grade students down to the library for a lesson from our young associate pastor. Like many associates in large parishes, Fr. Terry was fresh out of the seminary and harbored a deep passion for the Catholic faith.

That evening Fr. Terry taught our students about a prayer that he had learned while in the seminary. He and the other seminarians had prayed this prayer together each day, and it had remained an important part of his daily prayer life. Fr. Terry explained that the Angelus is prayed by many Catholics all over the world three times each day at the sound of bells ringing from church towers morning (traditionally six o'clock), midday (noon), and night (traditionally six o'clock). It takes its name—as does the Regina Caeli—from the first words of the prayer in Latin (*"Angelus domini nuntiavit Mariae"* and *"Regina caeli, laetare, alleluia"* respectively). We learned that the Angelus originated in the Middle Ages as a devotional practice for laypeople living near the great monasteries of Europe to help them follow the prayer example of those who lived monastic lives. The Angelus mirrored the regularly scheduled, structured prayer of the monks and nuns, who pause their daily work to recall salvation in Christ and to offer praise.

Fr. Terry explained that the Angelus is a Marian prayer, anchored by the recitation of three Hail Marys, but that it focuses our minds and hearts on the great mystery of the Incarnation. During Easter, he told us, Catholics set aside the Angelus and pray instead the Regina Caeli as a prayer of praise to God for the Resurrection.

This devotion had become for Fr. Terry a valuable and powerful way to pray, and he invited us to pray it with him.

I don't know how much of an impact that lesson made on my students, but I do know that his talk inspired in me an enthusiasm for prayer that I desperately needed. His talk gave new meaning to my experience in Rome years before. For the first time, I realized the significance of those Latin prayers. It was the first time in the five years since then that anyone had invited me to pray it with them. It wasn't a profound experience at first, but it sparked my interest. I wanted to learn more about the Angelus and how it could make an impact on a person like me. I decided that Advent to start praying this centuries-old devotion of the Church.

That's where my Angelus journey began. This book shows where it has led. I invite you to come along—to pray the Angelus with me and thousands of other Catholics around the world—and learn how it can make an impact on your life and the lives of the people you know and love around you.

The Angelus

V. The Angel of the Lord declared unto Mary.

R. And she conceived of the Holy Spirit.

> Hail Mary, full of grace,
> the Lord is with thee;
> Blessed art thou among women,
> blessed is the fruit of thy womb, Jesus.
> Holy Mary, Mother of God, pray for us sinners,
> Now and at the hour of our death.

V. Behold the handmaid of the Lord.

R. Be it done to me according to thy word.
> Hail Mary . . .

V. And the Word was made flesh.

R. And dwelt among us.
> Hail Mary . . .

V. Pray for us, O holy Mother of God.

R. That we may be made worthy of the promises of Christ.

Let us pray:

> Pour forth, we beseech thee, O Lord,
> thy grace into our hearts,
> that we, to whom the Incarnation of Christ, thy Son,
> was made known by the message of an angel,
> may by his Passion and Cross
> be brought to the glory of his Resurrection.
> Through the same Christ our Lord.
> Amen.

Regina Caeli

Queen of Heaven, rejoice, alleluia.

For he, whom you did merit to bear, alleluia.

Has risen as he said, alleluia.

Pray for us to God, alleluia.

V. Rejoice and be glad, O Virgin Mary, alleluia.

R. For the Lord is truly risen, alleluia.

Let us pray:

O God, who gave joy to the world

through the Resurrection of thy Son,

our Lord Jesus Christ,

grant, we beseech thee,

that through the intercession of the Virgin Mary,

his Mother,

we may obtain the joys of everlasting life.

Through the same Christ our Lord.

Amen.

An Invitation

This book is an invitation.

I am inviting you to join me in an ancient Catholic prayer practice called the Angelus. The Angelus is a daily Catholic devotion focused on the Incarnation of Christ. The call to pray the Angelus—still ringing in many church bell towers throughout the world—occurs three times each day, at dawn, midday, and at dusk. At 6:00 a.m., noon, and 6:00 p.m. Catholics around the world stop what they are doing and remind themselves of the presence of God in the world. They remind themselves that our great and all-powerful God became flesh. God became man. We are not alone.

I won't sugarcoat this invitation: praying the Angelus is a discipline. In order to reap the benefits of the devotion, you must commit to regularly praying it day after day. It is in the repetition and the fidelity that we receive the grace that God supplies through the practice. You are not likely to experience some great, awe-inspiring moment of divine revelation each time you come to the prayer. It is short. You begin reciting the words, and before you know it, you are finished.

Yet the devotion can be a source of tremendous grace. If you accept the invitation and stick with the practice daily, you will look back and find that God was indeed at work through the prayer. You will see that, although you may not have noticed it, he was pouring forth his grace into your heart little by little every day. He was making you worthy of the promises of Christ. In faith I trust that after many years of praying this prayer, we will be brought together through Christ's Passion and Cross to the glory of his Resurrection.

In the pages that follow, we travel into a deep meditation on the practice and contents of the Angelus and the Regina Caeli. These are meant to be communal rather than individual prayers. While you read, know that you and I will be praying together in spirit. And whether you are beginning the practice alone, as a family, or with a group, I encourage you to visit the website *The Angelus Prayer*, where you can connect with a virtual community of thousands of others across the globe who have made these profound and life-changing prayers a cornerstone of their Catholic devotional life.

In both practice and content, the Angelus meets us exactly where we need God's grace the most. Our culture escalates in us a desire to take control of our lives and determine our own destinies. Many of us are so focused on productivity that almost every hour of every day is scheduled and dedicated to accomplishing something. Work, for many people, is no longer contained within a nine-to-five workday: it follows us home on our devices. Those devices distract us continually, pulling us away from genuine interaction with the people around us at any given moment.

Praying the Angelus, on the other hand, reminds us to dedicate our time, our work, and our lives back to God. Each time we stop what we are doing and pray; we reorient our lives and our time toward God, the source of our lives and the inspiration for our work. In pausing to consecrate time back to God and rededicate our lives to him, we recognize that our life and our work are gifts that he has given to us and that we give back in return.

We do not, however, pray just any prayer three times each day; we pray to remind ourselves of many important truths about how God is present in our world. We repeat the words of the Annunciation and Mary's humble response to God's call; in doing so, we recall the Incarnation, the miraculous presence here on earth of our eternal God in the flesh—and the Incarnation brings irresistibly to mind the Paschal Mystery and the promises of Christ that we are living for today. We focus more intently on these promises during the Easter season, when we shift from praying the Angelus to praying the Regina Caeli, looking to Mary as Queen of Heaven and to Jesus who won for us eternal life by his Death and Resurrection.

Praying the words of the Angelus and the Regina Caeli can lead us to meditate on our daily lives. We can view our work and our calling through the lens of Mary's response to God's call through the angel Gabriel. We can reflect on our own response to God's call to us each day. We can offer up our lives and increase our awareness of the presence of God's Word in our lives and in our relationships with others. We can remind ourselves each day, as we worry about our time, that indeed our time here is limited and that we are meant for eternity.

In his apostolic exhortation *Verbum Domini*, Pope Benedict XVI summarized best the purpose of the Angelus: "This prayer, simple yet profound, allows us 'to commemorate daily the mystery of the Incarnate Word.' It is only right that the People of God, families and communities of consecrated persons, be faithful to this Marian prayer traditionally recited at sunrise, midday and sunset. In the Angelus we ask God to grant that, through Mary's intercession, we may imitate her in doing his will and in welcoming his word into our lives. This practice can help us to grow in an authentic love for the mystery of the Incarnation."[1]

Praying the Angelus is an act of openness to God's will. By stopping whatever we are doing and shifting our focus to him, we open our lives to his will and elevate its importance above our own desires of the moment. We can find great peace in our busy lives when we stop and remember that we are put here on earth to do God's will. Praying the Angelus three times each day reminds us that our lives are not our own. They are gifts, and we ask God for the grace to use them as he wishes—in ways we might never imagine on our own.

So, I invite you to join me and countless others in taking up this devotion each day. I invite you, also, to read and reflect on how the prayer may transform your life as you read the pages that follow. Finally, I invite you to use the meditations in this book to help you reflect more deeply on the words that we will be praying together. Let's begin.

Origins of the Angelus and the Regina Caeli

One of my favorite things about superheroes is their origin stories, which often distill their very essences as heroes. Batman is driven by the murder of his parents when he was a child; a desire for vengeance is often at the core of his heroic deeds. Spider-Man got his powers when he was a nerdy kid on a field trip. His intellectual nerdiness never goes away, and he carefully analyzes situations before jumping into action using his superpowers. Captain America was a scrawny young man before being given his super strength. This kept him humble as a hero.

These origin stories tell us about who the heroes are at their core. Just as the origin stories of comic book heroes reveal something of these characters' core identities, the origin and history of the Angelus reveals part of our core identity as Catholics. The Angelus developed out of our religious ancestors' ardent desire both to honor the role of the Virgin Mary in salvation history and to practice a devotion that made the grace of the Incarnation real.

Devotional practice is habitual, and many today criticize it as mindless and unproductive. Those of us who keep devotional practices, however, find that these devotions transform our days. The Angelus, which focuses on the Incarnation, orients us toward a deeper experience—not just a deeper understanding—of God's presence among us. Linking the devotion to fixed times—morning, noon, and evening—transforms daily life.

This is what our Catholic predecessors experienced as far back as the fourteenth century in praying the Angelus. Pausing three times each day to meditate on the Incarnation revealed God's presence in their daily lives. They were not seeking private revelatory experiences so much as an outward acknowledgment of their unity with Christ and with each other. The church bells would ring, and a community of people, though separated by space, was united through prayer and sacred time. The Word dwelt among them even as they went about the duties of everyday life.

When we pray the Angelus, we are united not only with others who pray this prayer each day, but with countless of the faithful over the centuries who have dedicated short moments of their day in unison with the whole Church to acknowledge and honor God's presence here on earth even today. The origin and history of the Angelus reveals that the unity and communion of our Church has its foundation in the Incarnation. We find unity in remembering Christ's presence here on earth today. God became man and dwelt among us during his earthly life not only to inspire us but also to unite us. Today, we rediscover this unity by meditating on the Incarnation each time we pray the Angelus.

Here are some of the key developments in the history of the Angelus and Regina Caeli devotions:

THE AVE MARIA (OR HAIL MARY)

Christian devotion to the Virgin Mary can be traced back to the earliest history of the Church. There are instances in the gospels that place particular emphasis on the Virgin Mary's importance in salvation: Jesus presents his mother to the beloved disciple from the Cross in the Gospel of John (19:26). Mary is present during Pentecost in the book of Acts (1:14). But it is Luke's account of the Annunciation, of course, that establishes Mary's place in the devotional life of the Church. From this story comes a wellspring of prayers entrusting the lives of the faithful to the aid of the Mother of God.

In the second century, St. Irenaeus took what St. Paul wrote about Christ as the Last (New) Adam (1 Cor 15:45) and showed that we could also look to Mary as the New Eve: "It was the knot of Eve's disobedience that was loosed by the obedience of Mary. For what the Virgin Eve had bound fast through unbelief, the Virgin Mary set free through faith."[2] This quotation shows that early Christians saw for Mary an important place within salvation history.

As time went on, including Mary in prayer became more common. The fourth-century saint Basil the Great is credited with writing, "O sinner, be not discouraged, but have recourse to Mary in all your necessities. Call her to your assistance, for such is the divine will that she should help in every kind of necessity." What words did Christians use through the ages in their recourse to Mary? They looked to the Gospel of Luke for inspiration for a prayer.

The Ave Maria, known in English as the Hail Mary, took on a devotional formula sometime in the eleventh century. It first echoes the words of the angel Gabriel during the Annunciation. His words praise Mary as "full of grace" and offer assurance that "the Lord is with" her (see Lk 1:28). These words are followed by the words Elizabeth said to Mary at the visitation: "Blessed art thou among women and blessed is the fruit of thy womb Jesus" (see Lk 1:42). The second half of the Hail Mary, our petition for her prayers, was added around the time of the Council of Trent in the sixteenth century and is not drawn directly from scripture.

THE POWER OF THREE

The three Hail Marys form the backbone of the Angelus prayer and also point to its beginning. During the Middle Ages, reciting the Hail Mary become commonplace; what is more, the practice of saying it three times became more and more prominent. The triple Hail Mary is often traced back to St. Anthony of Padua, who in the thirteenth century, taught his followers to "seek refuge in Mary . . . [who] provides shelter and strength for the sinner." Later in the thirteenth century, it is said that Our Lady appeared to St. Mechtilde, who called on Mary to assist her in her hour of death. Mary said to her, "I will, certainly, but I also want you to say three special Hail Marys to me every day."

Around the same time, Our Lady is said to have appeared to St. Gertrude the Great, saying, "To any soul who faithfully prays three Hail Marys, I will appear at the hour of death in splendor so extraordinary that it will fill the soul with heavenly consolation." The triple Hail Mary continued to be prayed and recommended by many other saints from the Middle Ages down through modern times, including St. Bonaventure, St. Stanislaus Kostka, St. Louis de Montfort, St. Gerard Majella, St. Alphonsus Liguori, and St. Josemaría Escrivá.

In the fourteenth century, the triple Hail Mary became a formal practice following Compline—the final daily prayer of the Divine Office or Liturgy of the Hours—in Rome. This action paved the way for this short devotion to take on a widespread appeal. Historical evidence suggests that the triple Hail Mary was said by the laypeople, who were illiterate and unable to follow along with much of the Office, as well as monks. At first, the recitation of the triple Hail Mary was associated only with Compline, but eventually the practice spread to the morning hour and later to noon as well. I hope you can see where I am going here.

ADDING THE ANGELUS

Sometime in the sixteenth century, the full text of the Angelus appeared in Catholic devotional books. Its earliest known appearance was in the *Little Office of the Blessed Virgin* in 1566. St. Peter Canisius published it in his *Catholic's Manual* in 1588. An ardent proponent of praying the Rosary, Canisius is also credited with adding the petition "Holy Mary, Mother of God, pray for us sinners" to the Hail Mary.

Aside from these early citations, not much more is known about the development and practice of the Angelus since it was a devotional practice and not a part of Eucharistic liturgies. For example, no one knows who first composed the prayer. The words, of course, are grounded in scripture (see Lk 1, Jn 1), but we will never know who first assembled them together with the three Hail Marys and concluding prayers. We do know, however, that the practice grew and became widespread in the centuries that followed.

The Angelus is a meditation on the meaning and importance of the Annunciation and Incarnation in our world today. The call and response prayers remind us of the faith of the Virgin Mary and petition her to pray that we experience the spiritual benefits of the Incarnation—to become more like her at the Annunciation and to experience more deeply the reality of the Incarnation that the angel's announcement initiated.

THE REGINA CAELI

The origins of the Regina Caeli are rich in history. In 1742, Pope Benedict XIV asked that the Regina Caeli be prayed in place of the Angelus during the season of Easter (Easter Vigil to Pentecost Sunday). While this is a more recent alteration in the devotion, the Regina Caeli prayer itself actually predates the current form of the Angelus.

While the authorship of the prayer is unknown, it is believed that Pope Gregory V introduced the Regina Caeli in the tenth century. Legend has it, though, that the prayer is much more ancient. As the story goes, another Pope Gregory, the sixth-century saint Gregory the Great, heard an angel singing the words of the Regina Caeli as he led a procession past the Mausoleum of Hadrian near St. Peter's Basilica during a time of extreme epidemic. The pope replied to the angel, "*Ora pro nobis Deum, alleluia!*" or "Pray for us to God, alleluia!"—part of the text of the Regina Caeli prayer we know today. The angel responded to the pope's plea by ending the pestilence that plagued the city. This is also one of the legends that explain the renaming of the Mausoleum of Hadrian to

Castel Sant'Angelo (Castle of the Holy Angel) and the nearby bridge to *Ponte Sant'Angelo* (Bridge of the Holy Angel).

Today, Catholics continue to pray the Regina Caeli in place of the Angelus during the season of Easter. Like the Angelus, it is a prayer that holds both Mary and heavenly angels at its core. Instead of focusing on the Annunciation and the Incarnation, however, this prayer focuses on the Resurrection and the joy of salvation. In this way, the two prayers act as bookends to our experience of Christ: he dwelt among us, uniting us together within his Church here on earth, and now he leads us to unity with him in everlasting life.

THE ANGELUS BELLS

To fully understand the tradition and history of the Angelus, one must know a little bit about the use of bells in Church history. Prior to the wide availability of clocks and watches, church bells had a couple of very practical purposes. The bells rang to announce the beginning of Mass, as they still do for most churches today. In earlier times, though, they were also used, especially in monasteries, to announce the times to pray the Divine Office. Throughout the Middle Ages, bells were rung even in parish churches for the morning Matins prayer and evening Vespers. As the practice of praying the triple Hail Mary and then the Angelus became more common, the bells became the means of calling both religious and lay-people to join together in prayer, no matter where they happened to be when they heard the tolling.

The bells themselves may reveal more about the history of praying the triple Hail Mary and the Angelus than official Church texts and prayer books do. As early as the thirteenth century, church bells bore an inscription of the Ave Maria. While some of these bells were dedicated to Mary, others were dedicated to St. Gabriel the Archangel. Even today we maintain this practice. As I write this, my parish is building a new church and bell tower. The tower will house four bells: one dedicated to Mary, another to the angel Gabriel, and two others whose dedication were chosen by a vote of the parishioners. Can you guess what the first two bells are going to be used for? That's right, the Angelus.

What better symbol could we have for the Incarnation of God than the bell? Think about it. If you are within hearing distance of a church bell tower, you have an almost constant reminder that you are always in the presence of God. I experienced this growing up in a house less than a mile from my Catholic church. Riding my bike through the neighborhood, I would hear the church bells ringing at various times throughout the day and think of God or at least be reminded of the place where I would go to pray to him. The same goes for my time in more recent years at the University of Notre Dame. The frequent ringing of the bells on campus didn't disrupt daily life; the bells were, rather, a constant reminder of what was nearby: a basilica that housed the Blessed Sacrament and where at regular times the university community gathered together to pray.

Ernest Hemingway even wrote a book with bells in the title that popularized a poem by John Donne. The poem reads:

> No man is an island
> Entire of itself . . .
> Because I am involved in mankind.
> And therefore never send to know
> For whom the bell tolls;
> It tolls for thee.[3]

Granted, the bells in the poem refer to funeral bells, but as I see it, all church bells toll for thee. They toll for all of us. While some of us now respond to the bells one, two, or three times each day to pray the Angelus or Regina Caeli, all of us can recognize in those bells a reminder of our unity no matter where we stand because we all hear them. The bells are also a reminder to us that Christ is present in the Blessed Sacrament in a church nearby. The presence of God is heard and felt through the beckoning toll of the bells.

How to Pray the Angelus

Praying the Angelus is very simple. It takes only a couple of minutes, three times a day. In fact, the prayer is more about the *when* than the *how* of the practice. At three specific times each day—dawn (six o'clock in the morning), midday (noon), and dusk (six o'clock in the evening) Catholics around the world stop whatever they are doing and recite the Angelus alone or in groups.

The prayer is anchored by three Hail Marys that are prayed after three paired scripture-based affirmations honoring the Annunciation and the Incarnation. The fourth pair of lines is prayer for Mary's intercession. These four pairs each comprise a versicle (call) (V.) and a response (R.), which can be either prayed by an individual or split between a leader (call) and a group (response). The Angelus concludes with a petition that God pour his grace into our daily lives.

During the fifty days of Easter, we set aside the Angelus to meditate and pray on the Regina Caeli, a prayer focused on the joy of the Resurrection of Jesus Christ and the hope that we may share with him in everlasting life.

Learning the words of the Angelus by heart takes a little time, but learning to integrate this prayer into your daily routine is by far the more challenging task. Today, we commonly live and work far from church bells tolling, reminding us to pray and so must set digital reminders on our phones, computers, or clocks. With these reminders in place, we simply need to commit to praying no matter what. We must decide that when that reminder pops up, we will drop everything and pray. Sounds easy, right? It is not as easy as you might think. It takes courage to pray the Angelus in public and discipline to pray it consistently even when you feel it hasn't made any impact on your life.

THE COURAGE TO PRAY

I wish I could say that praying the Angelus was immediately a profound and life-changing experience. It wasn't. I wish I could say it was easy. Instead, as with any devotional practice, praying the Angelus is hard. When I first began praying it during Advent years ago, I set up reminders on my phone. Then I downloaded an app that had the text of the prayer, which I was still learning at the time, and added another layer of notification on my phone. Easy enough, right?

I needed to actually stop what I was doing each time my phone buzzed with the call to the Angelus. This was a lot harder than I thought it would be. In the mornings, for example, I would be hard at work writing or researching. This often felt like the most productive time of my day. Sacrificing even two minutes of that time, especially when I was in the middle of work that had a deadline, was difficult. At noon I encountered a similar challenge: I would be at the office when the noon reminder popped up. Stop everything and pray? It felt risky. I work in a cubicle, so I was embarrassed. I was afraid my coworkers would see me as they made their way out for lunch and think I was either sleeping or—when I was still learning the prayers—overly obsessed with my phone.

But these weren't the only reasons I had a hard time getting started with this devotion, of course. The biggest reason I didn't consistently pray the Angelus in the mornings and evenings at first was that I was timid about sharing it with others, especially my wife. When I first started praying the Angelus, we lived in a small house. My desk was in the dining room/kitchen/sitting room. It was the same space where my wife worked in the early mornings. Inevitably when that 6:00 a.m. Angelus notification popped up, she was there with me in the room. Did I invite her to pray it with me? No, unfortunately I had some strange fear that I should keep it to myself. I felt as though she would think I had gone crazy-Catholic on her. I was trying to make the Angelus my own private devotion. I was reluctant to share it with others or invite them to pray it. Praying it privately just seemed like the more Catholic thing to do for some reason. It was a mindless, Catholic prayer, right? Who would want to pray it with me, let alone make the time to learn it?

I don't know exactly why I thought my wife, who is a devout Catholic, too, would think the Angelus was silly or see it as something too cumbersome to add to our days. I am glad I finally invited her to join me in the devotion. Today, I love our morning prayer time together. When she occasionally sleeps in and I pray the Angelus alone, I feel like something is missing. That short communal prayer time has increased our level of intimacy and become a great opportunity to witness our devotional life with our kids. If they wake up early, we invite them to pray, too.

DISCIPLINE YIELDS SPIRITUAL TRANSFORMATION

The consistent practice of any Catholic devotion takes a lot of effort. It's easy to give up. Whether it is the Angelus or another Catholic prayer practice like the Rosary, Divine Mercy, Stations of the Cross, or daily scripture reading, making personal prayer a habit requires considerable discipline.

Why? Because prayer usually isn't very fun. I know I shouldn't be writing that in a book that I hope will convince people to add a new prayer practice to their lives, but it is true. Many (perhaps most) people who take up these practices soon find disappointment and boredom in them. Feelings of peace, mercy, love, and certainty can often be present in daily prayer, but they are never automatic and often inconsistent. But we are, thankfully, not without consolation. Those who push through the sadness of not getting something out of every prayer experience find that over time the practice does form us spiritually.

For the first few weeks, even months, I didn't sense that I was getting anything out of praying the Angelus. I didn't feel a daily boost of spiritual graces or heavenly highs to get me through my days. Come to think of it, I don't think I ever felt an emotional response to the Angelus that kept me going and excited to pray it again in those early tries. Instead I had to rely on discipline and purpose to push through the temptation to skip the prayer. You will, too, if you want to experience the graces of this spiritual practice. What I realized over time was that the Angelus led me through a gradual transformation. I still don't feel this transformation every time I pray, and I don't think you will either. But praying the Angelus every day will change your life.

One thing I have learned for certain about Catholic devotional life is that you can't go into it expecting to achieve a specific goal. You won't necessarily get the result out of praying the Angelus or any other devotion that you hoped for. Sometimes, sure, you will experience what seems like a profound epiphany, but most days you won't notice anything is happening. Prayer is not imme-diately rewarding. It is not something we consume like food, drink, TV, or other forms of entertainment that make us feel good right away. The same thing can be said of the liturgical life of the Church: attending Mass does not always bring an immediately observable ben-efit, which is probably why so many people today don't like going.

I did not take up the Angelus hoping to solve a spe-cific problem or curb some specific bad habit. But through my practice of the prayer my habits did change, and the sinful temptations and tendencies in my life were made plain. Here's why: when you recite these same holy words again and again, they sink into your psyche. They start to reveal aspects of yourself that you did not real-ize were there or wish would go away. They describe the person you want to become. They point your inner com-pass toward a hidden goal that you will find yourself striving to reach.

A common exercise prescribed by motivational speakers and self-help gurus is to recite affirmations. Affirmations are statements that describe the per-son you want to be, the things you want to have or do. They paint a picture in your mind of what you want to become before you become it. By having that clear pic-ture in your mind, you start to notice opportunities to turn that vision into a reality. Devotional prayer has a similar effect. When we recite these prayers over and over again, they create a narrative in our subconscious of who we are meant to be with the help of God's grace.

The Angelus has the power to change you. That can be a scary thought, especially because you know that it won't change you all at once. With a thrice daily reminder of the humility of Mary, the Incarnation of Christ, and the glory that is in store for us, your life will slowly point in a new direction. It may take months of praying before you start to realize what God wishes to work in you through this devotion. It is my hope that this book will help you as you seek to uncover your own path through meditation on the Angelus prayer.

The challenge ahead is sticking with it. Most days—indeed three times *every* day—you will have to choose to stop what you're doing—no matter what—and pray the Angelus. This is the case for everyone who practices a disciplined devotional life. No matter who you are, whether a busy parent or a celibate monk, you will have to make the daily decision to continue the practice.

It never becomes easy. You should not expect to reach a point when you welcome the interruptive nature of praying at specific times each day. Trust me, though, you will thank me later. I thank God that he kept me interested in learning more about the Angelus and dedicated to adding it into my daily routine. Regular praying of the

Angelus has changed my life. Through discipline and perseverance, it will change yours, too.

What to Expect

I come from a family of both Roman Catholics and Southern Baptists. While my mom often worked during the weekend, I spent Saturday night with my Baptist grandparents. I spent a lot of time as a young boy going to the Baptist church and Sunday school instead of the Catholic church. When I eventually started to explore my Catholic roots and participate more intentionally in weekly Mass and Catholic prayers, I had a difficult time understanding the value of rote prayers, especially the ones that placed Mary in such high esteem.

The Baptist side of my family was very comfortable with prayer. They prayed all the time, and they never said the same prayer twice (other than the Lord's Prayer). With humble insertions of "we just" between petitions to God, my Baptist relatives prayed for God's help in a spontaneous way. As they observed me becoming involved in my Catholic faith, they began asking me to lead prayers. They assumed I was comfortable spontaneously praying aloud in small groups. But the truth was that I barely had any practice at all. This was not something I had practiced as a child in Baptist Sunday school and it was not something that I had the chance to practice often. I got more comfortable with praying spontaneously aloud in groups as time went on, but it wasn't something I did often as a Catholic.

If your family was like the Catholic side of my family growing up, then you did not take many opportunities to make up spontaneous out-loud prayers. My Catholic maternal grandmother said the Rosary, prayed the Hail Mary or the Lord's Prayer, and occasionally recited other memorized Catholic prayers that I did not recognize. My maternal grandfather had prayed the Rosary every day since fighting in World War II, but he did it so discreetly that I never even knew it until toward the end of his life. My mother and aunts and uncles also knew their Catholic prayers well because they had grown up praying them as a family and in Catholic school. Spontaneous prayer, however, was uncomfortable and seldom used. Before birthday dinners, holiday feasts, and big meals we would join hands, pause awkwardly, and say things like "Thanks for having [insert the name of the person whose birthday we were celebrating]" or simply "Thanks for having this." Looking back, this actually became a nice bonding moment for our family, but it showed some awkwardness that we felt praying together as a group. I only use it as an example of the striking difference between the prayer styles of my family's two faith backgrounds.

When I got older and started to learn about our Catholic devotions, I had a difficult time getting excited about them. I really appreciated the emotional power of spontaneous prayer whether it be alone or in groups. The Baptist side of my Christian upbringing told me that prayers should be prayed with passion and conviction. The Catholic devotions that were repetitive felt like empty recitations of words at first. I did not feel the emotion that I often associated with a "good" prayer session.

For many years after I embraced my Catholicism, I simply avoided Catholic devotional practice altogether. I often prayed silently before Mass, on retreats, before bed, etc., but I did not explore in great depth some of the traditional Catholic devotions. I carried a rosary in my pocket, but in all honesty, I didn't know how to pray with it. I mumbled my way through unique or uncommonly used Mass parts. In fact, I had to learn most of the traditional Catholic prayers like the Act of Contrition and the Morning Offering for the first time right along with my grade school students when I first became a Catholic school teacher. On the first day of school, I remember hoping that my students wouldn't notice that their religion teacher didn't know the prayers he was supposed to be teaching them.

So what changed for me? How can a Catholic with Baptist roots find so much joy in traditional Catholic devotions—especially ones with a special devotion to Mary? Let's go back to my first attempt at integrating the Angelus into my daily life. I think it will help you or anyone taking up a devotional practice again or for the first time. When I took up this devotional practice, I expected immediate results. I thought maybe God would show me some sign for my vocation just as the angel announced God's plans for Mary. I expected the devotion to make me a better person, more humble and less selfish. I expected to experience and see the fruits of my prayer as a concrete testament to God's grace in my life. I expected to feel all these things in my heart in a powerful and transformative way. I thought the Angelus would become the source of experiences I could share as a testimony to my faith.

Instead, I felt nothing. The Angelus reminder would pop up on my phone; I would stop what I was doing and pray, but most of the time I felt no internal change. So I would move on and continue to go about my day. I didn't give up on the discipline of the prayer, but I didn't believe I was getting anything out of it either. It took me months of daily practice just to begin realizing how God was at work in my mind and heart.

Over time and with dedication to the practice, I realized that God's grace was working in and through me in ways I had not expected. As I reflect on my experience and the conversations I have had with others about their experiences, I can list this series of spiritual lessons that those who pray the Angelus and Regina Caeli learn through the devotion:

- Repetitive prayer is more powerful than spontaneous prayer.
- Mary shows us how to live.
- Time is a gift from God through which he shows us our calling from moment to moment.
- We are called to be humble handmaids who serve others with our work.
- God reveals his will for us on his terms.
- God's Spirit is present all around us whether we realize it or not.
- The Resurrection of Christ is a source of great joy to be shared with the world.

Let's look at each of these lessons in greater detail. I hope that in reading this you will be convinced (if you haven't been already) to take up this practice of praying the Angelus and come to understand these lessons in your heart as well as your mind. Or, if you already pray the devotion, I hope these insights will deepen your prayer.

THE POWER OF REPETITION

I mentioned affirmations as a common exercise prescribed by motivational speakers. Visualization is another part of this process. Napoleon Hill, author of *Think and Grow Rich*, describes the practice of visualizing your success so concretely that your mind comes to expect it. Before you know it, you will reach your goal. His book, written during the Great Depression, has inspired countless people to use visualization to achieve not just financial success but physical, emotional, career, and even spiritual goals. According to Hill, "any idea, plan, or purpose may be placed in the mind through repetition of thought."[4] According to Hill, the more you repeat affirmations about who you are or visualizations about what you want to become, the more your mind leads you in that direction subconsciously.

The same principle applies to Catholic devotions such as the Angelus. After hundreds and thousands of recitations of "be it done unto me according to your word," you start to actually accept and welcome God's will in your life. After hundreds and thousands of affirmations that "the Word was made flesh and dwelt among us," you start to comprehend God's incredible gift of his presence among us today. The repetition of the prayer to the Mother of God enables you to take comfort in Mary's intercession. Grace will be poured forth into your heart not only because of your persistence, but because your mind and heart have been trained through repetition of thought to come to expect it. These are lessons that God reveals to us over time as we have trained ourselves to be prepared to see and welcome them in our daily lives.

This insight won't come to you in an instant; instead it will most likely be revealed to you as it was revealed to me over time. The repetitive praying of these prayers has changed me. The words of the prayers are burned into my psyche—they float in my head as an echo throughout the day. I am constantly comforted by them even when I am not pausing to pray.

WHOSE TIME IS IT?

There is more to the story. Along with this gradual training of the mind and heart through prayer have come moments of incredible shock when I realized that I wasn't living out what I was praying. It is humbling to admit these lapses publicly, but I hope it will be helpful to you.

Adding the Angelus to my routine has profoundly changed the way I see my early morning work time when I do my writing or work on my websites. I want to be very real with you here and share something that embarrasses me—a narrative of one particular morning while I was working on this book when the lessons of the Angelus hit me right in the heart. The experience was so potent that I had to write it down in a journal. Here is what I wrote to make myself remember what happened and how selfish I was:

> I woke up late this morning, but my daughters woke up early. This is *my* time. For several years now, I have set my alarm clock for 5:00 a.m. so that I can work on books, websites, and other projects that

I am creating before the rest of the family wakes up at 6:30. So when my time is interrupted with early requests for breakfast and questions about the day's events, I feel resentful. Why in the world are these kids up so early?!

I have so much to do and so little time. I can't possibly get it all done if I have to stop everything and tend to their every need. What am I, their servant? They make demands for waffles, toast, orange juice, and—oh wait—you forgot the vitamins! I go from resentful to angry very fast. Next thing you know, I'm yelling at them to say please and scolding them, saying "I am not your slave!" or "Just be quiet for one minute!"

All I want to do is get back to my writing. The thought picks me up a bit. There is some exciting work to be done. I have a book I can't wait to finish and a blog post that I know is going to make a difference in somebody's life. It's a calling—*my* calling—from God.

But then there is breakfast . . . and lunches. I haven't packed the lunches yet. Argh. I can't sit down at the computer

> now. The kids need my help. Forget the
> writing for today. This morning is lost.
> What a waste!

Sad, isn't it? I love my kids and I do want to serve them. Serving my family is the main thing I want to do in my life, really. Yet it is very easy to get caught up in another task or project we feel is so important that we ignore the needs of the ones right in front of us. That morning when six o'clock arrived and my phone reminded me it was time to pray the Angelus, I closed my eyes and prayed. My oldest daughter tried to get my attention: "Dad . . . Dad . . . Hey, Dad!" I'm ashamed to say that I neither stopped nor invited her to pray with me. Instead, I focused on the words and pretended she wasn't there— as if praying were some kind of escape from life.

That morning I missed the entire point of praying the Angelus. Unlike Mary, who responded positively to the interruption of an angel, I got angry at my kids for being there. Instead of embracing God's call as a handmaid and servant, I accused my kids of enslaving me and pulling me away from what I thought I was called to do. Instead of sharing my experience of Jesus, the Word of God, present among his people, I pretended my kids weren't there. I was the furthest thing from worthy of the promises of Christ.

GIVING TIME BACK TO GOD

A complaint I hear and often echo myself is that we just don't have enough time. There are not enough hours in the day. There's too much to do and not enough time. Time is something we want all to ourselves so that we can accomplish the many things we feel we need to do. The stress of not completing these projects can be overwhelming, so we begin to get grumpy. The stress piles up and we easily give in to anger. As others infringe on our "personal" time, we begin to resent them. We want our time to be our own and no one else's.

The Angelus, of course, is a prayer we say at specific times during the day. We don't recite the words whenever we want. Three specific times a day, we stop whatever we are working on wherever we are working on it and recite the prayer in unison with all others in our time zone. This practice flies in the face of that ownership we want to have over time. To stop and pray at specific times each day is to give those times back to God.

I think of my Angelus time as a sacrifice. It's always hard. I may be in the middle of writing an incredible sentence for a book when all of a sudden I have to stop mid-sentence and pray. This is truly a great way to show God that we know the time he has given us is a gift and that we choose to give it back to him.

You, too, will find opportunities to give your Angelus time back to God. Whether you are out in public or in a private place, stopping whatever you think is important in that moment and remembering that every moment is a gift from God is liberating. It frees you from being enslaved by work and opens you up to feelings of gratitude and appreciation for God's presence in your life.

THE CALLING OF THE MOMENT

Enclosed within the Angelus prayer is a paradox that all of us must grapple with throughout our lives. On the one hand, God has a plan for us. He is calling us to accept his grace-filled invitation to unite our will with his and embark on the journey he has in store for us. He sparks in us a passion for certain things and leads us to develop skills that we can choose to use wisely as we respond to his call. As a result, we frame within our minds a goal for the future. Many of us have uncovered a real mission in life or vision for the future and set out passionately to achieve that end.

At the same time, though, we exist in the present moment. There is a destination that God calls us to pursue, yet in the present moment we have many responsibilities to the people around us here and now. The paradox is that while we might be called to pursue a noble and distant goal, we cannot ignore the immediate needs of others along the way.

The tension between where we are and where we want to be can be excruciating. It causes people to work long hours or continuously check their phones. It leads people to frustration and even depression over their failure to make progress toward that goal. It causes relationships to suffer and can sometimes lead to separation.

I won't deny that all of us are given a calling by God. Just as he called Mary to give birth to the Savior of the world, God gives us a mission, too. Hard work and passionate pursuit of that mission are without a doubt two things God wants from us. At the same time, though, Mary didn't expect her calling. It was God's calling to her and not a well-formed plan she made on her own. She wasn't ready for it. She had to have the humility to accept the call and reroute her life in response to it.

How might we respond to the abrupt and unexpected interruption that the angel brought into the life of Mary? The angel of the Lord made his declaration before she even realized what was happening. I like to think she was in the middle of something very important to her when the angel showed up. No matter what you might be working on when the Angelus reminder rings, you will always think it is important. Praying the Angelus trains you to welcome interruptions as a possible gift from God. The interruptions to your day to stop and pray open you up to welcome other interruptions from friends, family, and neighbors.

I learned this lesson one workday immediately after the noon Angelus. I finished praying and shouted over the cubicle walls to my coworkers about whether anyone had the phone number of the closest Jimmy John's sandwich delivery store. I was getting hungry, and I had a gift certificate I was planning to use. Someone gave me the number, but another person asked for a Coke. *But I was going to use a gift certificate*, I thought. Rudely, I told her, "Sorry, I'm using a gift certificate." I was so set on my plan that I wasn't willing to allow an interruption. I wasn't willing to shift gears.

Rather than being present and looking for opportunities to serve those around me, I was focused on me and my plans. I realized almost immediately what I had done. I thought of the words I had just prayed, that I was supposed to be a handmaid who welcomed God's will. I went to my coworker, apologized, and said I would absolutely buy her a Coke. It wasn't even my money anyway.

WORK AS HUMBLE SERVICE

Praying the Angelus trains us little by little to be self-giving, humble, and holy. It slowly opens us up to God's grace within our hearts that transforms us and makes us into saints. I'm not perfect by any means, but I am grateful for the daily reminders that I should see myself as a servant and that my time is meant to be given away.

Our obsession with work extends beyond time. Our tasks, to-dos, and projects can become obsessions in themselves. There is a point at which our ambition and pursuit of even the boldest of callings overcomes our ability to see the needs of those around us. If we are not careful, we can prioritize our to-do lists over the people who really need us. Even if we would never say our work is more important than our family or friends, our actions and the way we relate to those we love often tell a different story.

In our society, people can easily become workaholics—those who suffer from an addiction to work, a step beyond the love of work into an inability to detach oneself from work. Today, with work accessible wherever we go through our phones and computers, it is all too easy for pressing work projects to intrude on personal time around the clock. We often hear the term "work-life balance" used in association with the workaholic culture we live in today. The idea is that we can manage our lives as a balancing of priorities between work and personal life (family, hobbies, leisure, health, religion, etc.).

In considering what this balance might look like, it helps to remember that work can be seen as a form of art. While we may not be painters or writers, we are still artists. In his book *The Gift*, Lewis Hyde defines art as a gift and not a commodity.[5] He writes about the process of creating art as an inspirational gift, bestowed on the artist, which is meant to be given to the world. The work of art endures whether or not it is bought. The artist does not create in order to get something in return. She simply passes on the gift of creation that she received. Whether we work on an assembly line, stay home to raise children, offer services as a business consultant, act as a receptionist, or have a career in law or medicine, our work is essentially a creation with value for others. It is a gift. We are mini-creators because of the work we do. We are artists, whether we realize it or not.

The Angelus reminds us where that creative force comes from: "And she conceived of the Holy Spirit." It is by the power of the Holy Spirit that we bring life to the work we do today. Unfortunately, our compulsion toward producing too often causes us to see our work only as responsibility. We feel we must accomplish the work at hand. We feel as though everything is riding on us. But the felt urgency to respond to the latest e-mail right away—or the world might just come undone—is a fallacy. The world does not rest on any one person's shoulders. The Angelus reminds us that all of our work is done through the power of the Holy Spirit and that we would be wise to recognize our work as a gift for others.

Mary's response to God's call also shows us a different mode of relating to our work by expressing a reality and vocation that we all share with her: we are all hand-maids or servants, and work is an expression of service. We serve God, of course, by doing his will, but we also serve others with our creative work. Work creates value for others and is always at the service of others. Taking on the mentality of a servant—rather than an employee demanding reward and payment—transforms the way we look at our work. Once we see work as an act of service, it is hard to justify focusing on work itself rather than on serving the people nearest to us.

Certainly there are times in which work and the rest of life necessarily grow unbalanced: an impending deadline or unavoidable business travel can make work matters pressing and time sensitive. But to be a workaholic is to skew the work-life balance perpetually and to let work consistently infringe on family and personal time and attentiveness. The work is not experienced as an opportunity to pass on a gift, but as an obligation to succeed; it is not coming from a place of service but from a place of selfishness.

After about a month of writing this book, I realized how far I needed to go in living what I prayed during the Angelus. My morning and noontime prayer sessions reminded me that my work is a calling from God, that my time is his gift to me, and that I—like Mary—should be always ready to serve both God and the rest of the world at a moment's notice.

Instead, I had let my to-do list become more important than the people in my life way too many times. I had responded to interruptions and requests from others with subtle resentment and eventually downright rudeness. I had let pride in my work become a sinful pride that pulled me away from God and isolated me from my family and coworkers.

Over time the Angelus has trained me to be more present to my family. When I am with them, I am better able to put the work or writing projects out of my mind. Family time is family time and not work time. Just as I learned to prioritize praying the Angelus in the midst of my work periods, I have learned to focus on family even when I am feeling inspired to complete some piece of writing.

The famous painting by Jean-François Millet called *The Angelus* expresses the proper relationship between work and God so beautifully. The two farmers have set their tools on the ground and bow their heads in prayer. The expansive field behind them clearly requires more work than they can possibly accomplish in a day. Yet they stop everything, set aside their work, and pray to God. The Angelus can conform us to this image so that we, too, can understand our work as a purposeful gift of service to God and to others.

DISCERNING GOD'S WILL WITHOUT EXPECTATIONS

When most people sit down to pray, they ask God to give them answers and expect to hear or see something in response. We've all turned to God when faced with a big decision—what career path to take, what college to choose, whether we are called to a religious vocation, or how to choose between two good choices (or bad choices). We pray about our needs and expect God to help us find an answer through some act of divine revelation.

In some ways, seeking God's guidance in this way is like praying for an angel to come and declare to us what we must do in life. We want answers, and we want them as soon as possible. This is one popular form of discernment, but the Angelus offers a different form.

In praying the Angelus, we meditate on an angel's unexpected visit to Mary, an event that Mary didn't plan or pray for. The angel did not bring her the answer to a question about her vocation that she'd been mulling over for weeks; she already had her life all figured out. Rather, God made his will known unexpectedly, and Mary responded in humility, turning away from the vocation she likely thought she had discerned.

Praying the Angelus, therefore, strengthens our practice of humility and openness to God's will for us. Its purpose is not to bring before God our difficult life questions.

Instead, it is a practice of openness and patience. We recognize that regardless of what we hope will occur in our lives, God has a plan. Just as he did with Mary, he may reveal a plan to us that is quite unexpected.

Imagine you are about to be married—or if you are married now, think back to the time just before your wedding. Think of all the dreams and thoughts for the future that a young engaged couple has. I imagine these same kinds of thoughts had been going through Mary's head before the angel Gabriel visited her. She must have been planning her wedding to Joseph. She would have been dreaming of the life they would share together in Nazareth and the large family they would bring into the world.

Then everything changed. God told Mary (and later Joseph) that he had a different plan for their lives. Mary was to give birth to a son named Jesus who would be the Savior of the world. Whoa. Talk about a life-changing U-turn! A new vision for the future was declared, and all of Mary's dreams about what she wanted to be and have in her life were shattered.

Like Mary, we who pray the Angelus wait in the hope that God's will be done through us. Through this daily, repetitive devotion, we begin over time to see his will unfold before us. Like Mary, we witness God's presence and work in our day-to-day lives through the good gifts he has given to us. When we take a few minutes each day to remind ourselves of God's presence in our lives, we find clarity not through long, introspective discernment but through the fluid reception of the day's events as they transpire. We come to recognize, by stopping everything and praying at the designated times each day, that God is working in our lives in unexpected ways and through whatever tasks keep us busy.

We are being trained to look for, welcome, and accept God's will in our lives. As the author of the Letter to the Hebrews writes, "You need endurance to do the will of God and receive what he has promised" (Heb 10:36). The more we see and appreciate his presence all around us, the more grateful we become for his working in this world. The more we pray about being handmaids and invite God's will to be done, the more we prepare ourselves to accept that will even in the most challenging circumstances.

Imagine, for example, that you are praying about how to handle a situation your son is having at school. You could pray in fear and worry about what to do and impatiently turn to God for answers. As a person who prays the Angelus diligently each day, however, you would be trained to be open to God's will. You would be more inclined to see God dwelling among us even in this worrisome situation. You might still feel fear and worry, but your confidence in God to carry out his will in this situation would be stronger. Even your decision to act would itself be grounded more in the hope of being a handmaid than in an attempt to be the master and controller of the situation. You would experience the added comfort of knowing that God, whose Spirit dwells among us, is by your side even in this most challenging situation.

Granted, none of these benefits is automatic. The benefits of praying the Angelus each day derive both from the grace God gives us within the act of our prayer and the subconscious training of our minds and hearts—the formation of our souls through the repetition of thought and word—to truly live what we pray. Am I more patient and willing to accept God's will in my life than I was before I began praying the Angelus each day? I hope so. I know for sure that every time I am faced with a big decision, the words of the Angelus echo in my brain: *declared, handmaid, be it done unto me, made worthy,* etc. The Angelus can be a powerful discernment tool.

ANGELUS MOMENTS

As you settle into praying the Angelus regularly, you will start to experience what I call "Angelus moments." These are times when God expresses his will for us in the events of our daily lives. These are moments in which we can practice the spiritual lessons of the Angelus. Here are some examples of Angelus moments:

- You are deeply entrenched in a project at work. Things are going well. You are rolling along and checking things off your to-do list. Then a coworker stops by and asks for some help. You are right in the middle of something. If you stop now, you might lose your train of thought. Your coworker needs help now, though. You set your project aside and go assist in whatever way you can.

- It's the end of a long day, and you are just about to sit down and relax for the evening with your favorite TV show. Then the phone rings. It's your sister. If you answer, you are probably going to have to talk for a half hour or so. So much for that relaxing TV show— you've got to be there for her. You pick up the phone and listen.

- It is the middle of the night when your crying child wakes you. You tend to him and calm him down. He's back asleep, but not for long. Ten minutes later he's crying again. You calm him and put him back to sleep again. Soon he is up again. This goes on for a couple of hours. By the fourth or fifth time, you are exhausted and feel like you can't take any more, but you don't give up. Eventually, he calms down, thanks to you. Sleep never felt so good.

- The office you work for is closing. You haven't lost your job, but you are going to have to relocate to a new city. This will have an enormous impact on your family. But all is not lost—there is a lot of potential in your new location. There will be an adjustment, and no one wants to leave your current home, but you can see the possibilities awaiting you.

In each of these situations, it would be easy to let anger or resentment ruin the experience. In each situation, a comfortable, familiar plan was in place when a call to change direction and serve came. Angelus moments are opportunities to set aside our plans for ourselves—to reject our selfishness—and serve God and others instead.

REJOICE, ALLELUIA!

This brings me to the final lesson of praying the Angelus. Through both the discipline and the content of the prayer, the Angelus redirects our hearts and minds toward God. By intentionally interrupting whatever we are doing when it's time to pray the Angelus, we grow increasingly aware that no matter what we are doing, God is present. He is not distant and uninvolved in the world today. He is present and his Spirit can be felt within us and all around us. God is the center of our existence and is ultimately more important than any big or little activity in which we are engaged when the Angelus bell tolls.

We haven't said, though, what we get in return. What happens to us if we let the Angelus transform us? What gift might we receive?

The answer can be found most clearly in the Regina Caeli, which we substitute for the Angelus during the fifty days of Easter. The message of the Regina Caeli is a message of joy. We join Mary, Mother of God, Queen of Heaven, in rejoicing over the Resurrection of her son. How great and wonderful it is! Is there anything else in this world that matters when compared to this awesome gift of new life? Despite so much doubt and despair in the world, we can rejoice in knowing that, because of the Resurrection, even death's power over us has been shattered. We have been set free.

A brief survey of the lives of Catholic saints reveals people of great joy, especially in difficult circumstances. The joy of the saints has almost always come with struggle and reliance on the assistance of the Lord. Mary herself experienced great sorrow at the suffering and death of her son, yet we can barely fathom the great joy she has in his Resurrection.

As Christians who practice devotions such as the Angelus and Regina Caeli, we find joy in unlikely places. We let the sometimes boring repetition of prayer and devotion fill and change our hearts over time, although we do not always experience feel-good emotions along with it. We practice our prayer, discovering that the joy of everlasting life is to be found in our relationships with those who need us most and in the everyday activities of our ordinary lives. If we are open, we can see that God is present here with us today. We have so much for which to be grateful, and because of that gratitude, we are compelled to give back and serve those around us. The more we escape the selfish pursuit of our own desires, the more we can spread the joy of the Gospel to those who may lose hope without it.

Our willingness to set aside our plans and assist those around us can be a source of great joy for us and for others. The more we become attached to our plans, routines, and habits, the less we can serve others. In the isolation that results, we may reach our goals, but we will not find joy. Joy only comes in the unselfish love and service of others. We can only experience the joy of the Resurrection if we are open to sacrificing ourselves as Jesus did. Through unselfish, sometimes painful service, we, too, can know the joy and glory of new life in Christ.

In commitment to the consistent practice of praying the Angelus and the Regina Caeli, we find joy. We find joy in the silencing of our will and the consequent openness to God's plans for us. We find joy in the gifts of God's presence in our lives and in the grace given to us throughout each and every day. We find joy in our newfound ability to recognize and receive that grace and in accepting our responsibility to proclaim our joy to the world in which we dwell.

Why Pray
the Angelus Today?

As I close this introduction to the Angelus, I want to place it in the context of the larger cultural milieu in which we find ourselves in the twenty-first century. The devotion, though centuries old, is unknown to most people in the Church today. Yet after years of experiencing it daily, I am convinced that there has never been a more important time for us to pray the Angelus than right now.

PRAY WHAT WE PREACH

The "New Evangelization" is a term used by recent popes and now many other Catholic leaders to address the need to engage those who have already been baptized in the Church yet remain distant from it and from Christ. It is a call to evangelize within—to reach those who consider themselves Catholics but who have neither a personal relationship with Christ nor any deeply rooted connection to the Church.

At the core of the New Evangelization is the challenge for us to present the Gospel, which is unchanged over the millennia and is often perceived as old and irrelevant to our lives today, in new and fresh ways. So much of what people think they know about the Catholic Church is misunderstood; ancient Church teaching must be re-presented in new ways that capture the true essence of our faith. The Angelus is one traditional practice that I believe meets our culture exactly where it most needs transformation and conversion. It is the spirit of the New Evangelization that sparked my desire, in fact my *calling*, to write this book.

In preparation for writing this book, I met with Dr. Timothy O'Malley, author of *Liturgy and the New Evangelization* and director of the Center for Liturgy at the University of Notre Dame. Tim and his colleagues at Notre Dame's larger Institute for Church Life (ICL) gather along with a number of graduate and undergraduate students to pray the Angelus at noon each weekday. The ICL, in fact, has become so dedicated to encouraging the Angelus devotion that they included it as one of the three core devotions in their popular mobile app, 3D Catholic (http://3dcatholic.nd.edu).

Tim and I discussed the spiritual fruits of our individual practices of this devotion, and then our conversation turned to the importance of the Angelus within the context of the New Evangelization. At the time of our talk, my book about evangelization, *To Heal, Proclaim, and Teach*, was about to be released. The premise of that book is that our efforts to evangelize must include efforts to heal the marginalized and proclaim the Good News instead of almost exclusively focusing on efforts to catechize and teach Catholic doctrine in traditional faith formation programs. Tim challenged me to look closely at prayer in the context of evangelization. In pointing out to me the essential role of devotional practice and popular piety in evangelization, Tim helped me see an aspect of evangelization that I had not fully considered.

Pope Francis makes the same point in his 2013 apostolic letter on evangelization, *Evangelii Gaudium*: "We are called to promote and strengthen [popular piety], in order to deepen the never-ending process of inculturation. Expressions of popular piety have much to teach us; for those who are capable of reading them, they are *a locus theologicus* which demands our attention, especially at a time when we are looking to the new evangelization" (126).

For example, Tim shared with me his thoughts on religious education. Parents, he pointed out, are asked to be the primary teachers and catechists of their kids when children are baptized. For the most part, Catholic religious education programs for children have a heavy focus on conveying doctrine. The catechetical leaders, catechists, and teachers expect parents to help their kids learn those doctrines at home. Many parents, however, have not truly been evangelized and are poorly catechized. They do not feel comfortable teaching about doctrines because they are not confident enough in their knowledge of Church teaching to be able to explain things well enough to their kids. Even those parents who

attended Catholic schools as children often feel inade-
quately prepared to pass on Catholic teaching effectively
to their own kids. Rightfully so, they look to the Church
for help.

In *Evangelii Gaudium*, however, Pope Francis describes
nearly the opposite scenario when writing about parents
and popular piety. He writes, "I think of the steadfast
faith of those mothers tending their sick children who,
though perhaps barely familiar with the articles of the
creed, cling to a rosary; or of all the hope poured into
a candle lighted in a humble home with a prayer for
help from Mary, or in the gaze of tender love directed
to Christ crucified" (125). He imagines a mother praying
for her child with deep devotion and heartfelt love for
Christ. She may not be well catechized, but she certainly
has been deeply evangelized. Her devotional prayer is a
form of proclaiming the Gospel without direct teaching
or preaching.

What if, instead of concentrating almost exclusively
on passing on our doctrines to our children, we gave an
equal or even greater focus to passing on and practicing
devotions? Which is easier to ask of parents: to pray a
specific prayer at specific times each day (before meals,
before bed, at the hours of the Angelus) or to have an
in-depth conversation about Catholic doctrines with
their child each day? Which is better: for parents to accurately explain to their children what the Church teaches

about the Sacrament of Penance or for parents to show them its importance by going to confession themselves?

I know so many families today that catechize their children at home more through their devotional practice than structured lessons. They go to Mass. They pray with their children before meals and bedtime. They spend time volunteering at their parish in various ministries or during liturgies. They pray the Rosary as a family (or a decade of the Rosary at least). They may even pray the Angelus. Why? Because the example we show as parents through prayer is a more powerful form of passing on our faith than any kind of forced lesson or conversation about what we believe.

It is time that we collectively place a renewed emphasis on practicing what we preach rather than just preaching—or more accurately, just teaching. Whether you work and volunteer in a parish or are simply a devout Catholic disciple, you can practice your faith through participation in the sacraments and observance of Catholic devotions. In my opinion, there is no better devotion to practice than the Angelus, a devotion that is intimately ingrained in our daily lives and thus has the power to transform us day by day.

PRAYER WOVEN INTO DAILY LIFE

Let me illustrate this point in another way. Islam is the world's fastest growing religion, yet many of us

Christians know little about it. Have you ever seen a Muslim pray? I was in New York City for a conference a few years back and experiencing my first time staying in the city as an adult. The first evening I was there I set out on a little tourist expedition to see St. Patrick's Cathedral and then Times Square. When I got to the cathedral—which was mostly empty—I found myself a pew, said a brief prayer, and then walked around for a while examining the architecture and the shrines to the saints in the back. I then grabbed a St. Jude prayer card and headed out to see the lights of Times Square. What I saw on the way, however, touched me more deeply.

It was a quiet night, and the street I took was relatively empty for downtown New York. Almost hidden off to the side of the sidewalk was a man on his knees. He was standing, bowing, and kneeling down for *Salah*, the act of worship Muslims perform at five specific times each day. He was inconspicuous—not flashy or overbearing. He was not in the way of pedestrians and yet not hidden either. The dedication this man had to his religion was very moving, an inspiration to me, and further convinced me to turn toward habitual prayer in my own life. Not long after that night in Manhattan I first learned about the Angelus from a priest in our home parish—a Christian prayer that, like the Islamic *Salah*, is to be consistently practiced at specific times each day.

Rather than pointing to the ideological "isms" that oppose Christian belief as the cause of Christianity's decline, I wonder if it would be more accurate to say that Christian culture has declined from within due to the widespread abandonment by Christians of a habitual devotional life. I believe that we Catholics suffer today from a laxity in prayer: most of us do not structure our days around prayer. It is not that we have failed to live up to some kind of outwardly imposed obligation. It is that many Catholics do not attempt and therefore do not experience the spiritual benefits of a structured devotional life. A regular devotional life is seen by many as something only for the über-Catholics. That was how I felt before I began practicing the Angelus; I was more in favor of emotion-rich spontaneous prayer. I thought prayer was best when we made up the words on our own. I thought we had to feel emotionally inspired to pray. Now I see that the more we integrate structured devotions into our day, the closer we are to God and the more we are formed into the saints we are called to become.

We must become better at sharing the richness of our Catholic devotions and not just our Catholic doctrines. We must become better at practicing these devotions in public and inviting others to join us. This change cannot be effected only through more books, or faith sharing groups, or lecture series, or faith formation nights focused on Catholic devotions. Instead, we must spread the devotions by keeping them ourselves and letting them evangelize us.

When we say the word "amen," we declare that the words we have heard or said are true. Our minds may not always be pondering the great theological depths of the words we speak when we pray the Angelus and the Regina Caeli, but our proclaiming "amen" at the end reaffirms that we declare the truth of those words. We bear witness to this truth by committing to pray the prayers each day. Our devotional life, filled with amens, affirms our faith in God, in his Church, and in the doctrines which reveal in greater detail the Lord that we encounter in the prayers we proclaim.

I hope the meditations that follow will help your amen take on new meaning each time you pray. I hope these words will inspire in you the desire to let the grace that God has poured into your heart ignite both a passion for seeking his will and perpetual gratitude for all that he has given you. May we find unity in this common practice and meet one day in the glory of the Resurrection.

Angelus Meditations

In the second and third parts of this book, you will find brief reflections that are meant to inspire personal meditation on each phrase of the Angelus and the Regina Caeli. These may be used as weekly reflections throughout the year or read each day and recalled as you pray. You can also read them at your own pace and in isolation of the daily practice. My hope is that these reflections, whether read intermittently, all at once, or in bits and pieces, will inspire deeper meditation on how the words that you pray make an impact at this particular moment in your life. Returning to the meditations will foster a deeper understanding of each phrase and, more important, a deeper grasp of the meaning that these phrases have for each day.

The Angelus

V. The Angel of the Lord declared unto Mary.

R. And she conceived of the Holy Spirit.

> Hail Mary, full of grace,
> the Lord is with thee;
> Blessed art thou among women,
> blessed is the fruit of thy womb, Jesus.
> Holy Mary, Mother of God, pray for us sinners,
> Now and at the hour of our death.

V. Behold the handmaid of the Lord.

R. Be it done to me according to thy word.
> Hail Mary . . .

V. And the Word was made flesh.

R. And dwelt among us.
> Hail Mary . . .

V. Pray for us, O holy Mother of God.

R. That we may be made worthy of the promises of Christ.

Let us pray:

> Pour forth, we beseech thee, O Lord,
> thy grace into our hearts,
> that we, to whom the Incarnation of Christ, thy Son,
> was made known by the message of an angel,
> may by his Passion and Cross
> be brought to the glory of his Resurrection.
> Through the same Christ our Lord.
> Amen.

The Angel of the Lord Declared unto Mary

IMAGES OF ANGELS

When you think of angels, what is the first thing that comes to your mind? For many of us it is an image of a half-dozen plump babies with wings smiling down from their clouds in heaven. They are cute and adorable (but—let's be honest—also a little bit creepy).

If not babies, you probably pull up an image of a winged adult clothed in white. Think about that image for a moment. Would you describe paintings of Michael and Gabriel as feminine or masculine? Do they appear in your mind almost like cartoon princesses? Most people's version even of the celestial warrior Michael the Archangel has the face of someone who would not hurt a fly.

After seeing countless depictions of angels as babies or fairy princesses, we may lose our understanding of an important characteristic of God's messengers: they inspire fear. When Mary sees Gabriel for the first time, she is frightened. The angel has to comfort her, telling her not to be afraid. In fact, this is what angels do throughout the Bible whenever they appear to people for the first time.

When the angel declared God's will for Mary, she could not have taken it lightly. Yet she listened and accepted God's will that she would conceive his son despite all the fears that must have come with her acceptance of that responsibility. Likewise, we should never expect God to communicate his will for us in ways that do not frighten us at least a little. Coming to an understanding of God's will for our lives is almost always fear-inducing whether it is perceived as good or bad. Are you afraid of what God might be calling you to be and do? This just might be that angel to be feared in your own life.

Meditation

Picture in your mind an image of an angel. What does the angel look like? Is this an angel that would inspire fear such as Mary experienced? Reimagine this mental picture in such a way that you feel wonder, awe, and even fear at the sight of the angel.

GOOD MESSENGERS

Although they don't have much in common in English, the words "angel" and "gospel" are very similar in Greek. The word "angel" in Greek is *angelos* or *aggelos*, which means "messenger." The word "gospel" descends from a direct translation into Old English of the Greek *euangelion* or *euaggelion*, which means "good message" or "good news."

Both angels and the Gospel have the same effect on the people that come in contact with them. They both bring God's message into the world and inspire a personal transformation. Whereas the angel delivered one particular good message to Mary, Mary enabled the entire world to hear the good message of salvation (the Gospel) through her son, Jesus Christ.

Today, we are God's messengers bringing the good message to the world. We carry out God's will by sharing the Good News of God's presence here in the world. May we, like the angel Gabriel, speak with confidence as we share this good message, the Gospel.

Meditation

At the end of each Mass, the priest or deacon commands us to "go forth." The next time you hear those closing words, consider them a calling—just like the angel's declaration to Mary—to go out into the world and share the Good News.

THE NEW EVE

It is hard to think of the story of the Annunciation without thinking of the story of creation, in which a fallen angel appeared to Eve. Just as St. Paul called Christ the "Last (New) Adam" (see Rom 5:12–14, 1 Cor 15:22), early Church Fathers dubbed Mary the "New Eve." St. Irenaeus wrote, "The knot of Eve's disobedience was loosed by the obedience of Mary. For what the virgin Eve had bound fast through unbelief, thus did the Virgin Mary set free through faith."[6]

Hidden within the Angelus—such a short and simple prayer—is all of salvation history, beginning with Adam and Eve and finding fulfillment in Christ and Mary. Looking back to the beginning helps illuminate Mary's place in the story. While Eve succumbed to the lies of the devil, Mary resisted her fear and doubt and embraced the truth that the angel declared. Mary could easily have talked herself out of this calling just as Eve allowed the serpent to talk her into eating from the tree of knowledge. Instead, Mary made a choice that enabled God himself to come into the world and undo what was done by Adam and Eve. Through Mary's cooperation, God completed his plan for our salvation.

Meditation

When there is something in our lives we know we should do but are afraid of doing, we often try to talk ourselves out of it. That voice in our heads rationalizes and makes excuses just like the serpent in the creation story. When you experience such moments, do you listen to that rationalizing voice in your head?

THE DECLARATIVE

Look closely at the first chapter of the Gospel of Luke. The angel speaks in declarative sentences. A declarative sentence, you might recall from your English classes, differs from imperative sentences (commands), exclamatory sentences (strong feelings), and interrogative sentences (questions). A declarative sentence simply makes a definitive statement. The angel doesn't express strong feelings or ask questions. He doesn't give commands. He makes definitive statements about God's will and his work in the world. He has not come to Mary with a request. He has come to her bearing the good news of God's work in her life and the life of her cousin Elizabeth. He *declares* unto Mary.

How does God communicate with us? Is he asking us questions? Is he giving us commands or making requests? What if, instead, God communicates his will for us in the declarative? When you think of a God who declares his will rather than requesting our response, you start to understand the power of the Incarnation. God is here. He is with us. He is active and working in the world whether we are aware of it or not. May we have the courage to let his will be done to us according to his Word.

Meditation

Are you open to God's declaration of his will in the world, or are you resistant to the destiny he is making known? Pray for the courage to accept and welcome God's will, to let his will be done in you.

And She Conceived of the Holy Spirit

LIKE GODS

Let's consider further the connection between Eve and Mary. Eve gave in to the temptation of the serpent and believed his false promise that she and Adam "will be like gods" (Gn 3:5). Eve craved that power and chose to take it for herself despite God's warning. With the words of the Angelus, we recall the way in which God's plan for the redemption of humanity unfolded. In an act of incredible humility, Mary let herself be overcome by God's power. She did not seek to become like a god but rather allowed God to work through her. Mary conceived, and God the Son was born into the world through the power of the Holy Spirit.

The Holy Spirit can only work in our lives when we are humble and open to God's will over our own. When we welcome the Holy Spirit into our lives, we allow God to work through us, and we find joy, peace, and fulfillment. We become in this way like Mary, who brought Christ into the world. If we grasp, like Eve, at success, glory, and the things we selfishly want for ourselves, then we reject the work of the Holy Spirit. If we try to be godlike through our own efforts, we fail every time. Without the Holy Spirit, our life loses meaning and joy.

Meditation

Make two lists. Label one list "I Want To Be in Charge" and the other list "God Is in Charge." Be honest about what areas of your life you categorize under each heading. Once you are done, think of ways you can open yourself up to moving the items on your list over to God's list.

GIVER OF LIFE

In the Nicene Creed we profess our faith in the Holy Spirit, "the Lord, the giver of life." This is actually the second time we mention the Spirit in the Creed. Earlier, we recall that Jesus Christ "by the Holy Spirit was incarnate of the Virgin Mary, and became man." What does this Holy Spirit do according to this proclamation of faith? The Spirit gives life.

When we echo the words of the Creed and declare the Spirit's power to create life during the Angelus, we might take the time to reflect on God's work in our world today. God, the Holy Spirit, is the giver of life. Two people, with the help of the Holy Spirit, joined in union together to form another human life. Parents never fully plan or control when conception occurs. Conception is a true gift. Couples who struggle with infertility would offer anything to receive that gift and those who experience unplanned pregnancy can likewise see conception as something they cannot fully control. It is the Spirit that gives life.

The Spirit's work in the world extends beyond conception. We use words such as "lively" and "spirited" to describe happy, passionate people. When we embrace life with joy and excitement, we are filled with the Holy Spirit. The Spirit gives us life not only at conception but also today and every day that we welcome God's presence in the world.

Meditation

Are you filled with life today? Why or why not? Have the courage to open yourself up to the presence of God and the working of the Holy Spirit in the world at this moment.

CREATIVE INSPIRATION

Artists, writers, actors, comedians, and other creative people will tell you that they do not know where inspiration comes from. They sit down and work. Sometimes inspiration strikes and something beautiful is created. Sometimes inspiration doesn't arrive and the art they make is less satisfying. Artists don't have to be religious in order to come to the realization that inspiration has a spiritual, uncontrollable nature. Knowing they are not making the art all by themselves is what can make artists humble. Art is created in unity with something deeper, something subconscious and difficult to describe. The artist's role is to humbly accept creativity and inspiration when it arrives and bring art into the world.

This is how the Holy Spirit, the giver of life, works in the world. Each day we pray the Angelus, we affirm the Spirit's power at work in the world. Mary did not create Jesus, but neither was she merely a vessel. The Spirit worked through Mary, and Mary was filled with the grace to accept her role in bringing Christ into the world. Like Mary and like the artist, we, too, can accept the creative inspiration to bring something amazing into the world.

Meditation

What act of creation is the Spirit working to create with and through you today? You do not have to be an artist or a writer to experience inspiration. What ideas and actions are you feeling compelled by but unsure if you should bring about right now? May we have courage, like Mary, to respond to God's inspiration.

Behold the Handmaid of the Lord

BEHOLD, BE BOLD

We don't use the word "behold" very often in conversation; it is usually reserved for dramatic moments in movies or books. It is a word we might hear announcing something great and magnificent. "Behold" suggests something powerful and incredible and amazing. You would never use this word to draw attention to yourself in regular conversation, right?

Well, Mary does, but in a unique way. She doesn't respond to the angel with an announcement of her greatness as the future Queen of Heaven. Instead she proclaims, "Behold *the handmaid of the Lord*" (see Lk 1:38). Behold the handmaid? The very idea of beholding a humble servant is so counterintuitive. Yet Mary embraces her humility and expresses with great passion her willingness to serve God wholeheartedly. At this moment, her very soul is proclaiming the greatness not of her own gifts but of the Lord.

In artwork depicting the Annunciation, Mary is nearly always depicted with such a quiet, serene, and timid look on her face. This imagery falls short of capturing the boldness of Mary's response to the angel. To the angel's announcement in Luke 1:31 that "Behold, you will conceive in your womb and bear a son," Mary responds with that same level of authority and graceful power to "behold" her as a humble yet awe-inspiring handmaid of the Lord.

Be bold in your commitment to humility in life. Like St. Paul, boast in your weakness and dependence on God (see 2 Cor 12:1–11). Only God can create goodness in the world through you.

Meditation

All of us want to have complete control over some areas of our lives, areas we resist entrusting to God. Whether it is a career path, a relationship, or a bad habit in your life that you are holding on to, be bold in your commitment to deny yourself and turn that part of your life over to God. It will be scary at first, but with this commitment and trust in God comes a great gift of peace that can never be obtained on our own.

THE HANDMAID CINDERELLA

The most well-known story of a handmaid is the classic tale of Cinderella. A young lady's father dies, and she is left in the power of her evil stepmother and mean stepsisters. The king of the land throws a ball to find a bride for his son, the prince, among the young women in the kingdom. Everyone will attend except Cinderella, who is left at home to complete chores instead. Cinderella's fairy godmother comes to her aid and sends her to the ball in splendor and beauty. There she meets the prince, and they fall in love. They part as the evening ends but are reunited after the prince matches her abandoned shoe with the young lady. The handmaid becomes the royal maiden —a beautiful princess and the future queen.

Now, set Cinderella side-by-side with the Virgin Mary. Mary chooses to be a handmaid. It is through her choice to serve that she is elevated to queenship, not in this world but in the next. There's no royal ball or beautiful dress. There is no fairy godmother to transform her into someone she is not. No, she accepts who she is and proclaims the greatness of the Lord without any mention of her own gifts of beauty or stature. Mary is completely filled with the love of God and empties herself in service to him.

How do we find our happy ending? Follow Mary's path rather than Cinderella's. Don't wait for your fairy godmother to show up out of the blue and transform you into someone who will impress others. Instead, humbly embrace God's gifts in your life and vow to serve him with joy. Give thanks and offer your service to God. That is the Gospel path to the kingdom of heaven.

Meditation

Are you hoping God will be your fairy godmother? Are you hoping that someday he will magically whisk all your problems away? Instead, choose service over earthly rewards, that your treasure may await you in heaven. Recognize how God has already been active in your life, and think of special ways that you can respond by serving him today.

BECOMING HANDMAIDS

When we meditate upon the Angelus, we put ourselves into the stories and prayers that we recite. We imagine ourselves as Mary as we speak her words: "Behold the handmaid of the Lord. . . . Be it done unto me according to your word" (Lk 1:38). This is the only phrase of the Angelus in which we recite an actual person's words. Elsewhere, we tell parts of the Annunciation and Incarnation and pray with one another for Mary's intercession.

I find it fascinating that we take on Mary's persona in our prayerful journey to become more like her. Each time we pray her ancient words, we make them new and unite our current thoughts, troubles, hopes, dreams, and worries to them. Each time we declare ourselves to be God's handmaids and proclaim our openness to his will, we invite his presence into our lives in a new and different way—and we are called to serve him and those around us in a new and different way.

Meditation

How is God calling you to be a handmaid today? Is it as a parent or a spouse? Are you to be a handmaid to your boss at work or to the customers you serve through your job? Are you to be a handmaid in your parish? Are you to be a handmaid to the strangers you see or meet today? Or are you to be a handmaid directly to the Lord? Consider who God is calling you to serve today, and make a special effort to serve with joy.

Be It Done unto Me According to Thy Word

FROM FEAR TO TRUST

We have such a funny relationship with God's will. Much of the time, we know what God wants us to do, but we're afraid that it won't make us happy. When we resist God's will, we almost always have other plans in place that we are afraid to lose. We want things done our way. Pope Francis addressed this state of affairs in a 2013 Twitter post: "Sometimes we know what we have to do, but we lack the courage to do it. Let us learn from Mary how to make decisions, trusting in the Lord."[7]

Mary "was greatly troubled at what was said" according to the Gospel of Luke; in fact, the angel had to comfort her: "Do not be afraid" (Lk 1:29–30). Her fear then turned to doubt: "How can this be?" she asked the angel, who reassured her that "nothing will be impossible for God" (Lk 1:34, 37).

When we have big decisions to make in life, we should expect to feel that fear at first. We should even expect, like Mary, to enter into periods of doubt about the possibility of God's will for our lives will become a reality. Ultimately, like Mary, we can turn to God in loving trust when faced with difficult choices. We may not know what the future holds, but we can be confident that God's love for us is much greater than we can understand.

Meditation

Do you have any decisions that you are unsure of or afraid to act upon? You may know in your heart what you have to do. Pray for the courage to act. Decide, and place your trust in the Lord, just as Mary did.

BEING VS. DOING

My wife tells me of a theology class she had in high school that was entirely focused on prayer. She jokes that the students used to love the days when their teacher would take them down to the chapel to just "be" in prayer. She laughs that they liked to use that "being" time as nap time. As teenagers, they just didn't see the point of it.

With our busy lives and many responsibilities, we tend to be constantly active. Every free moment, waiting in line at the grocery store or on the way to and from meetings, people are on their phones. Our work hours are packed. During our free time, we perpetually feel the need to be doing or planning something to do. If time were an empty jar, we would constantly be filling it up.

Mary shows us a different way. We don't know what she was doing when the angel appeared to her. We do know, however, that she was open to what God planned. Mary didn't respond to the angel's declaration with a command: she didn't say "Do it" or "Make it so." She was much more receptive than that. She said "Be it done" or "May it be done" (Lk 1:38). In that phrase we find her willingness simply to let something be done. Mary, in response to the angel's message, did not feel compelled to do but chose simply to be.

Meditation

Take some time today to consciously refrain from "doing" and focus on "being." Sit in silence and clear your mind of everything except Mary's simple words "Be it done." Refrain from any thoughts of working or praying harder, and just sit in God's presence for a few moments. As you go about your day, practice the art of simply being present in the midst of your busy day and resist the urge to be constantly active.

MARY'S FIAT

Mary's words "May it be done" or "Be it done" are often referred to as her *fiat*, which is the first of these words in Latin. Mary's fiat is her submission to God's will. When we echo her words during the Angelus, we, too, submit to God's will in our lives. We model our faith after Mary's faith opening ourselves up to the will of God.

Why is Mary such a great model for faith? It all goes back to her fiat. With full trust in God, she set her will aside and let his be done. Think about the choices she had. She could have said "Let it be done later," and she could have downright refused—but she didn't. As a result, God brought redemption into the world through Mary.

God wants to bring life, peace, and goodness into this world through you, too. Are you willing to let it be done? Have the courage to echo the words of Mary and live the life God wants you to live.

Meditation

Is there a fiat you need to make today? Think through your day. When have you needed or will you need to submit to God's will for your life? Pray for the strength to echo Mary's words and let it be done.

GETTING PICKED

Remember when you lined up as a kid to get picked to be on a team in gym class or during recess? It was always a nerve-wracking experience. You didn't want to get picked last because that would mean you weren't as good as the other players. You wanted to be one of the kids to be picked first, high-fiving your all-star teammates and relieved that you were good enough to be with them.

Imagine how Mary felt. She got picked. What an honor! She must have been filled with excitement and, at the same time, fear of letting God down. Despite her nervousness, though, she didn't turn down her chance to be on God's team.

God has picked you. It doesn't matter now whether you were picked first to be on the soccer team at recess as a kid. Right now, God is picking you for something. What is that something? It is likely a task or role you are good at and enjoy. What are you passionate about giving back to the world?

Are you ready to let God pick you? It is harder than it seems. We're not always willing to accept honors bestowed on us by others—even by God. Follow Mary's example. Be honored. Let God pick you. Respond by answering his call and letting it be done according to his word.

Meditation

In what area of your life do you feel God is calling you to something great? Visualize God picking you like a kid waiting to join a team at recess. Look around. Who is on your team? What are you going to accomplish together?

And the Word Was Made Flesh

IN THE BEGINNING

In this part of the Angelus prayer, we turn to a different gospel. We move from Luke's account of the Annunciation to the opening of the Gospel of John: "In the beginning was the Word, and the Word was with God, and the Word was God. . . . And the Word became flesh and made his dwelling among us, and we saw his glory, the glory as of the Father's only Son, full of grace and truth" (Jn 1:1, 14).

Luke shows the connection between Mary/Gabriel and the creation story with Eve/Satan, while John repeats the introductory words of Genesis ("In the beginning . . .") to connect the Incarnation with the seven-day creation story. Both gospels give us a sense of the eternity of God as well as the incredible miracle and gift that is his coming into the world as an infant.

These words from John's gospel are an important reminder of who Jesus was and is. He was not "created" in the Incarnation; he has always been and always will be. He was there in the beginning and he will be there in the end. He came into this world in flesh and blood so that we could share in his eternity.

What does that reality mean to us as we pray the Angelus? It challenges us to recognize God's presence among us. Even if we cannot "see" him in the flesh, we can still see his glory all around us through the gifts of his creation and through the relationships we have with other people.

Meditation

Our God, the God who created us, became human. His gift of creation is gift enough; his gift of becoming one of us is beyond understanding. Practice gratitude today by supplementing your Angelus with a prayer of gratitude to God for creating us and for becoming one of us.

LOGOS

John opens his gospel with an important Greek word, *Logos* (Word), which is a concept from Greek philosophy that is packed with meaning. By equating Logos with Jesus Christ, John makes an important connection between who Jesus is and the contemporary Greek conception of Logos.

Logos, in Stoic philosophy, could refer to a universal principle of reason. The word *logic* has its root in Logos. The Greeks also associated Logos with creation as the underlying force that animates the world. In that sense,

God did not create the world as a potter creates a pot. Rather God is the animating force that not only made but sustains creation. Creation is not a set reality, so much as an ongoing state of existence. God is creator, and we are the created, in ongoing relationship.

What does this mean for our understanding of Christ? Why did St. John the Evangelist use the concept of Logos to open his gospel? Because it expresses the fact that even though Jesus was a human, he is not only a human. His divinity stretches beyond space and time. God is the rational force—nothing fantastical—that animates and gives us life. During the Angelus we recall that Christ became flesh, but that Incarnation didn't inhibit his eternal existence. He still dwells among us in each one of us, holding us in existence.

Meditation

Consider praying for those who live according to reason alone, without faith. Find joy in the fact that the divine Logos is with them and animates them and their lives, too, even if they do not realize it.

THE FLESH

In St. Paul's New Testament letters, he often writes negatively about the flesh. He writes, "For I know that good does not dwell in me, that is, in my flesh. . . . For I do not do the good I want, but I do the evil I do not want" (Rom 7:18–19). We can all relate to this. We all sin. We all do things we know we should not do or fall into addictions that are hard to break. Most of these temptations and addictions have to do with bodily urges for food and sex. While not evil in themselves, temptations of the flesh can become easy doorways to sin.

We are, however, not without hope. God himself became flesh like us, sharing that same flesh that leads us so easily into sin. What an incredible gift! Yes, like St. Paul we continue to do that which we do not want, but we are not lost. Because Christ became flesh, he redeemed the flesh. Through his grace, he enables us to break free from bondage to sins of the flesh and gives us the power to rise above our temptations.

Meditation

What are the temptations, addictions, and bad habits that afflict you? Recognize that our God became flesh to redeem us and save us from the evil that our flesh leads us into. As you pray the Angelus each day, ask Jesus for the grace to choose good over evil—to overcome your biggest temptations and break free from the bondage of sin.

BOW YOUR HEAD

When we recite the Creed on Sundays, we bow our heads in unison when we say the words "and by the Holy Spirit [he] was incarnate of the Virgin Mary, and became man." Likewise, during the Angelus it is customary to bow our heads or genuflect when we say "And the Word was made flesh and dwelt among us."

Why do we bow? Bowing, of course, is a sign of humility and respect. You would bow to royalty. In some cultures, you bow as a form of greeting to show respect. You bow to your partner at the end of some traditional dances.

During an Angelus address in 1979, St. John Paul II spoke about bowing our heads. *Inclinate capita vestra Deo!* ("Bow your head before God!"), he began, referring to the exhortation to bow our heads on Ash Wednesday. He went on to explain the meaning of bowing the head: "Bowing the head before God is a sign of humility. Humility, however, is not identified with humiliation or resignation. It is not accompanied by faint-heartedness. On the contrary. Humility is creative submission to the power of truth and love. Humility is rejection of appearances and superficiality; it is the expression of the depth of the human spirit; it is the condition of its greatness."[8]

So, without shame or resignation, with both humility and courage, we bow before God made flesh. We recognize that our greatness comes from this place of humility. God humbled himself to become flesh like us; we humble ourselves to become like God.

Meditation

Whether you are praying the Angelus right now or not, bow your head. What feelings or thoughts immediately arise? When we bow our heads, we are likely to be bowing to someone, submitting to someone. Think of that someone (God) to whom we bow. He is worthy of our submission. Take a few minutes to think about why we owe God the submission of our will, our thoughts, our very lives.

And Dwelt Among Us

EMMANUEL

One of the most popular Advent and Christmas hymns is "O Come, O Come, Emmanuel." *Emmanuel* is a Hebrew word meaning "God-with-us." The song expresses our longing for God. We are in exile here without Christ; we are lonely and isolated without God.

But even today God is with us! We remind ourselves of this every time we pray these words of the Angelus: "The Word became flesh and dwelt among us." We don't have to be alone. God is present here even today. Our God is not distant and unknowable. He is present among us and working in this world even if we do not have him in the flesh anymore.

What an incredible gift that our God did not remain far off but became one of us. Through his mercy and love, God took on our flesh to be one with us. He shows his love for us by offering us his very life and his presence with us today. Though we cannot see him in the flesh, we can find comfort in knowing that he is not far off. We can experience his presence in prayer or in adoration before the Blessed Sacrament. We can recognize his presence and working in the world in each moment of our day. We can meet him in the face of strangers and friends that we encounter each day. God is here today. God is with us.

Meditation

As you pray the Angelus today, think of the emotional drive behind the song "O Come, O Come, Emmanuel." Hum the tune in your head. You might even pray the words of the Angelus to that same tune. As you do, consider the hymn's desperate plea for God to be with us. At the end of your prayer, give thanks that God continues to dwell in you and in your life.

GOD DOES NOT HIDE

One of the most famous movie quotations in recent decades comes from the film *The Usual Suspects*: "The greatest trick the devil ever pulled was convincing the world he didn't exist."[9] There is a lot of truth to this claim. In fact, C. S. Lewis expressed a similar sentiment in *The Screwtape Letters*, writing as the fictional demon Screwtape: "I wonder you should ask me whether it is essential to keep the patient in ignorance of your own existence. . . . Our policy, for the moment, is to conceal ourselves."[10]

To take this idea a step further, it is safe to say that the devil has done a great deal more than conceal himself. He has completely concealed from many people the existence of any spiritual beings. Many people have accustomed themselves to the idea that since they cannot see God, angels, or demons, these spiritual beings do not exist.

Christians not only believe that God is real, but that he took a human form and dwelt here with us on earth. People saw him, touched him, ate with him, and then shared their stories of him as witnesses to his existence. These stories were passed down from one disciple to the next and recorded in the gospels. Jesus appointed his Apostles, and they ordained bishops and priests to form a chain of witnesses to testify to God's true presence here on earth. God does not conceal himself the way the devil does. He took bodily form and dwelt among us with nothing to hide.

Meditation

Imagine that you were one of the disciples at the time of Christ. Imagine that you saw Jesus with your own eyes and believed him to be the Messiah. What would you have to say about him? What would you want to communicate to the world about who he was and, in particular, who he was to you?

I AM WITH YOU ALWAYS

At the end of the Gospel of Matthew, Jesus leaves his disciples with some parting words: "I am with you always, until the end of the age" (Mt 28:20). In the Angelus, we proclaim that the Word was made flesh. We remind ourselves that Jesus was and is Emmanuel, "God-with-us." He was made flesh but remains with us and among us today. His parting words are a reassurance to us all that he will always be with us, dwelling among us, even if we cannot see him.

Pausing each day and reciting the words of the Angelus help remind us to look for Jesus' presence among us today. How is he with us? He is within us. He is within the people we meet and encounter each day. He permeates the natural order. He is all around us. Jesus Christ, the Word made flesh, is with us today—and the way we see the world changes day by day.

Meditation

As you proceed through your day today, look for God's presence. Do you see God in the people around you? Where do you find hints of his presence in the day's events? Do you experience God's presence in the natural world?

Pray for Us,
O Holy Mother of God

PRAY FOR US

So often we pray for people other than ourselves. We seek the good in and for others and appeal to God to shower his graces on them. When we need prayer and ask others to pray for us, we feel great consolation and reassurance. Hearing "I'll pray for you" from someone makes us grateful that we are not alone. United in prayer, we can find comfort not only in God's care for us but in the support of others.

At the same time, we can be limited by the number of people we confide in for prayers. We may have a large community of support, or it may be that we have only a few close friends and family that we can turn to for prayer. As Catholics, though, we can go further: we can appeal to the angels and saints to pray to God on our behalf. We may not hear a response, but we can feel confident that if we ask a humble saint for his or her help, our plea will be heard.

If this isn't reassurance enough, we can find solace in our ability to turn to the Mother of God herself to intercede for us. Read that again: the Mother of God. We can ask the Virgin Mary, the Mother of God himself, to pray for us. And she does, every time we ask. In the Angelus, we ask her to pray for us every day each time we pray. That, I hope, is some consolation in good times or bad. God's own mother is praying to her son on our behalf.

Meditation

Spend some time today either during the Angelus or in between prayers to bring specific needs and prayer requests before the Mother of God. Ask for her prayers for these specific needs, and be comforted in her willingness to present them to her son, our Lord Jesus Christ.

THEOTOKOS

God has a mother. Let that sink in for a moment. He has a human mother. It is a powerful concept. The very idea threw the Church into a heated debate that led many to break into their own factions outside of the Church in the fifth century. To believe as we do that the holy, infinite, and all-powerful God would humble himself to be born as a son of a human being is nearly unbelievable. Yet that is exactly what God did. He chose a human mother here on earth to give birth to him.

In this part of the Angelus we echo that audacious Greek name for Mary, *Theotokos*, Mother of God or more literally, "God bearer." We ask her to pray for us, that we may be made worthy of her son's promises. Thanks be to God that he made this worthiness possible: our God became man so that man could become like God. Through his humility, our unworthiness can be transformed into greatness. Our God was so humble that he took a human mother.

Think about your own mother for a moment. Whether you are close with her or not, mothers are an integral part of all our lives; we all feel—or at least we long to feel—great affection for mothers. Our God looked upon Mary with this same affection on earth and still does in heaven. This is why we seek her intercession.

Meditation

In your prayers today, turn to Mary to intercede on your behalf. Ask for the strength to live out the humility of Christ and be made worthy of the promises he makes to us.

That We May Be Made Worthy of the Promises of Christ

WE ARE MADE WORTHY

We all find ourselves sometimes in situations in which we feel unworthy. This feeling of unworthiness might arise when we are asked to join a committee at our parish or our kids' school, or when we are hanging out with a new group of people or in a new social situation. We can feel unworthy while spending time with people who are more skilled than we are, more talented, more experienced, or more comfortable doing something important.

How do we get past that feeling of unworthiness? In most of these situations, we realize over time that we were actually worthy all along. We had nothing to worry about. The same goes for our relationship with God. We can take on misguided attempts to make ourselves worthy through hard work or self-effacing pain when really it is God who made us and makes us worthy. By God's grace we will continue on our way to Christ's promise of everlasting life.

Meditation

In what areas and situations in your life do you feel a sense of unworthiness? Think deeply about the source of that sense of unworthiness. Is it a fear of rejection? Offer that fear to Mary, the Mother of God, to bring before the Lord on your behalf. Allow the Lord to fill the void that those feelings of unworthiness create inside of you.

Pour Forth, We Beseech Thee, O Lord, Thy Grace into Our Hearts

POURING FORTH

Think of all the other words we could have used in the Angelus to ask for God's grace: *give, hand over, deliver, grant, bestow, bequeath, pass out.* But none of these words quite captures the meaning of "pour forth." There is some distinct imagery here, and it has two parts.

First, we ask that grace be *poured* into our waiting hearts, not given as an object to be received. From this metaphor we learn that grace, like water, must be held in something. It cannot be carried alone like a package. It flows and fills. Grace flows into our hearts and, if we are open to God's will, is held there.

Second, grace is poured *forth* from God, not just poured. The extra word reminds us that grace has its source in God. An often used image is that of grace overflowing out of God and into us. So grace isn't just some really good thing; grace is the gift of God himself. It is his life poured forth into our lives.

Now that we have received God's grace, the pouring continues: we share that grace. It pours forth from us.

Meditation

As you pour yourself a drink today—whether it is water, coffee, or something else—observe this "pouring forth" from the faucet or pitcher closely. Think now of God's grace pouring forth and filling the cup of our hearts. What will you do with that grace today? Will you let it be poured forth into the lives and hearts of others?

A HEART FULL OF GRACE

In the Hail Mary, we echo the words of the angel to Mary, whom he calls "full of grace." Here at the end of the Angelus we turn to God and ask that he fill us with grace as well. Notice what we ask God to fill with his grace: our hearts. This is so that we, like Mary, may love God back completely. It was God who "first loved us" (1 Jn 4:19), and we wish to love him back.

Grace is a free and undeserved gift. We hope that, filled with grace, we will be able to reciprocate with a free, completely deserved gift of our love back to God. Think about what God has done for us. He came to this earth and lived among us, he died, he rose, and he remains with us today. That is grace. That is the love of God made manifest. We ask that our hearts be so filled with grace that we can give it right back to God.

Meditation

Has anyone ever given you a gift that you didn't ask for or think you deserved? You felt as though you owed that person something, right? You either gave a gift in return or sent a thank you note. Think about all the undeserved gifts you have received from God. How can you give something back to God or say thank you to him in creative ways?

That We to Whom the Incarnation of Christ, Thy Son, Was Made Known by the Message of an Angel

IN THE FLESH

Paper cuts are painful. Biting your tongue can be excruciating. Stubbed toes, a stinging funny bone, chapped lips—our bodies can sustain all sorts of little annoying and painful injuries. While small, these pains can dominate our days if we let them, distracting us from what is really important in life. We can easily become complainers.

This is the bodily state that our God chose to take on for himself. God became incarnate (meaning "in the flesh") and everything that comes with it. He experienced for himself all those little, annoying pains as well as far more serious pains during his passion and death. Why? To redeem them. Every pain, no matter how annoying, finds new meaning in Christ.

How? Christ shared in that pain, too. He felt pain just as we feel pain today, no matter how great or small. Any pain, no matter how annoying, finds new meaning in

Christ. Think about it. Every time we experience some bodily pain, we can recall that our God endured it, too.

Meditation

Think about your body right now. Are any small wounds or pains bothering you? Try the old practice of "offering it up." It used to be a common practice among Catholic parents to tell their complaining children to "offer it up," meaning offer up your pain for the souls in purgatory. This practice helps us and those for whom we offer up our pain because we recognize that our Lord, too, experienced pains just like ours and worse. In this way, we unite our pain with his. We are not alone in the pain that comes with being fleshly creatures. God became flesh, too, and experienced that pain just like us.

FROM ANNUNCIATION TO INCARNATION

It is easy to focus more on the Annunciation than on the Incarnation when we pray the Angelus. The Annunciation is easy to imagine. It is much more concrete. We can picture the angel and Mary and the conversation they had with each other.

The Incarnation, however, is difficult to visualize. What do we picture in our minds when we consider the

Incarnation? Do we think of baby Jesus? Do we think of grown Jesus walking around on the earth, preaching and teaching about the kingdom of God? Do we ponder the intricacies of the Trinity? Meditating on the mystery of the Incarnation can be a real challenge.

Although flesh is concrete, the Incarnation itself is an abstraction—maybe the most abstract of ideas, because the thought of God becoming man is so strange. God, who is immaterial, eternal, and omnipotent, could and would not possibly become one of us, right?

Yet he did. The Incarnation is a beautiful mystery and one worth remembering and pondering every day. While it may be easier to meditate on the Annunciation during the Angelus, we cannot forget that our real focus should remain on the Incarnation of Christ, which is what the angel came to announce.

Meditation

What images come to your mind when you think of the word "Incarnation"? Write them down as they come to you. Don't try to come up with some abstract idea to ponder. Instead, focus on the specific images and thoughts that come to mind and spend time considering each one. You may find new and unexpected perspectives on the Incarnation as you do.

May by His Passion and Cross Be Brought to the Glory of His Resurrection

THE ONLY WAY TO GLORY

How do we get to the glory of the Resurrection? The closing prayer of the Angelus reminds us that it is only through Christ's Passion and Death that we are brought to the glory of his Resurrection. That does not match up with how the rest of the world seeks glory, does it?

Many people today tend to glorify the lives of celebrities, actors, musicians, athletes, and successful businesspeople. Paparazzi feed our craving to see the latest photos or hear the latest scandal or gossip about these people. News media focus on headlines and stories that draw the attention of those who just can't wait to hear what is happening in the lives of the people we place on pedestals. Many people, whether they realize it or not, like to watch these celebrities fall. It is as if they want to be reassured that their glory is not enduring, that celebrities are really just as flawed as we are.

The Christian faith paints a different picture of glory; it tells us that glory comes only through suffering and death—death to ourselves, death to selfishness. If we seek the glory of the Resurrection rather than the glamour and glory of this world, we will find ourselves seeking to suffer on behalf of others. We will follow Christ on a path of sacrificial love—the path to true glory—the glory of the Resurrection.

Meditation

What images of glory have been ingrained in your mind through popular culture? Ask yourself honestly what type of glory you have been seeking. Do you seek glory through sacrifice and death to self as the Angelus calls us to do?

REFLECTING ON LENT

We pray the Regina Caeli during Easter since it celebrates the Resurrection, but we pray the Angelus during all the other liturgical seasons. While we might say that it is especially relevant during Advent due to its focus on the Annunciation and the Incarnation, it does contain a perfect tie-in with the season of Lent.

The Angelus closes with a testimony to the Passion and Cross of Christ. After focusing on the beginning of Jesus' time here on earth, we remember his end. The mystery of the Incarnation cannot be isolated from the Passion and Death of our Lord, for it is not through the Incarnation alone that we find salvation but through Christ's saving work in the Paschal Mystery. His complete self-sacrifice leads us into grace. His humiliation opens the path to glory.

The Paschal Mystery is a traditional topic for Lenten meditation. We remember that our God loved us so much that he died for us. We remind ourselves that the true path to glory is the path of the Cross. We give of ourselves and give up all attachments so that we can grow closer to Christ. Through this humility come joy and the glory of the Resurrection. The Angelus makes for a wonderful Lenten devotion because it promotes detachment ("Be it done unto me") and selfless serving of others ("Behold the handmaid of the Lord") and keeps our minds on the Paschal Mystery ("[may we] by his Passion and Cross be brought to the glory of his Resurrection").

Meditation

Think about what you gave up during the most recent (or current) season of Lent. Relate that sacrifice to the words of the Angelus. How did you live out (or are you living out) the words we pray during the Angelus by making that sacrifice during Lent?

A SUFFERING SERVANT

The Old Testament prophet Isaiah wrote of the Lord's Suffering Servant: "I am honored in the sight of the Lord and my God is now my strength" (Is 49:5). As Christians, we can turn toward the Cross denying ourselves and experiencing suffering in order to find strength in God. We do not suffer for suffering's sake. When we take up our cross and serve others, we make their lives better. We make them happier and we become happier as a result.

When we follow Christ to the cross, suffering takes on new meaning. Through our own choice to suffer for others, we are strengthened and supported by God. The Angelus is a reminder of this crucial fact that God is with us especially in our suffering. We find the glory of the Resurrection through the pain of humble service. Thankfully, we are not alone. God accompanies us through this suffering. He is our strength. We are always with and supported by God.

Meditation

When we do something kind for another person, it makes that person feel good. It makes us feel good, too, especially when we aren't seeking any special recognition from others. Do something kind and unexpected for someone today, maybe even a stranger. Don't ask for anything in return. Seek glory and honor only in the eyes of the Lord, who sees what you have done even if no one else does.

Through the Same Christ, Our Lord. Amen.

THROUGH AND THROUGH

"Through and through" is a common phrase that means "thoroughly, completely, or in every aspect." I like that. I think this phrase adds deeper meaning when we end each prayer with "through Christ, our Lord." Think of the entire world completely offered through Christ; every aspect of our lives and our world offered through Christ. Christ is both the center and limit of our entire world.

We conclude this prayer about the Incarnation recognizing that even the prayer itself is offered through Christ. Everything we say and do exists within and through Christ. We do not reside on some distant part of the universe where God can't be found. He is here with us. He is among us. He is present.

And so we offer our prayer through him who is completely with us in every aspect of our lives. Through him we turn over to the Father all our troubles, our worries, and our hopes.

Meditation

Is there any part of your life that you feel the need to keep separate from God? Is Christ thoroughly and completely involved in every aspect of your life? Think of those areas that you can offer back to God, then offer them through Christ, your Lord.

AMEN

Have you ever wondered why we say the word "amen" at the end of a prayer? Sure, it serves as a nice conclusion to any prayer. It lets people know that the prayer is over. It adds a communal element so that everyone gathered can proclaim amen in unison even when we are not the ones actually saying the prayers.

But what does it mean? Jesus said amen repeatedly to introduce many of his teachings: "Amen, I say to you . . ." In Aramaic the word *aman* means "be confirmed, supported, or upheld." In Hebrew, the word *emet* means "that which is true, dependable." Some Bible translations, therefore, have Jesus introduce his teachings with "Verily, verily" or "Truly, truly." "Amen" is used to confirm the truth of and support something that is stated. In much of the southern United States it is common practice for people in Protestant (and some Catholic) congregations to shout amen in support of powerful preaching statements. Even in common conversation people will say "Amen to that" or "Amen, brother" to confirm something is true.

So, why do we say amen at the end of a prayer? We do so as an affirmation that what we have prayed together is true. In Catholic liturgies, the congregation joins in saying amen even when the priest offers a prayer on their behalf. Likewise we end the Angelus with an amen. We conclude by proclaiming that our recitation of the Angelus wasn't just a mindless ritual—it was a proclamation of a truth so deep it is worth praying again and again each day.

Meditation

The next time you say amen, whether after the Angelus or after another prayer, think of the real meaning of the word. With your whole heart and mind proclaim that what you prayed is true—that you confirm and support what was said.

Regina Caeli Meditations

Regina Caeli

Queen of Heaven, rejoice, alleluia.
For he, whom you did merit to bear, alleluia.
Has risen as he said, alleluia.
Pray for us to God, alleluia.

V. Rejoice and be glad, O Virgin Mary, alleluia.

R. For the Lord is truly risen, alleluia.

Let us pray:

O God, who gave joy to the world
through the Resurrection of thy Son,
our Lord Jesus Christ,
grant, we beseech thee,
that through the intercession of the Virgin Mary,
his Mother,
we may obtain the joys of everlasting life.
Through the same Christ our Lord.
Amen.

Queen of Heaven, Rejoice, Alleluia

THE HUMBLE QUEEN IN THE KINGDOM OF HEAVEN

When Jesus was asked about the place of the apostles in the kingdom of heaven, he said to them, "Whoever wishes to be great among you shall be your servant" (Mt 20:26).

This declaration makes Mary's place in the kingdom much easier for us to understand. She lived a life of complete service to and love for God. She opened herself up to God's will in her life and always stayed in the background. Look closely at her role in the gospels, in Acts, and even in the letters of the New Testament; she is rarely the focus of attention. Instead, the attention centers on her son and on the work of the Holy Spirit in this world. She lived out what she expressed in the Magnificat (see Lk 1:46–55), proclaiming the greatness of the Lord and not her own.

As we meditate on the mysteries of Christ's Resurrection and our path to everlasting life, it is good to constantly remind ourselves what kind of kingdom we are heading toward. Those who are last will be the first. If you want to be great in heaven then make yourself a servant—a handmaid—to others.

Meditation

In what areas of your life do you find yourself trying to outperform or outdo others? In which areas do you seek to put others before yourself? Think for a moment about how you feel about both areas of your life. Which makes you happy? In which do you find fear and worry? Seek happiness through service to others.

CORONATION OF MARY

The final Glorious Mystery of the Rosary concentrates on the crowning of the Virgin Mary, Mother of God, as Queen of Heaven. I tend to imagine a royal celebration in her honor: the trumpets of angels blaring and lots of bright lights and heavenly bliss. It is hard not to think of medieval coronations.

Mary, though, is a queen unlike the queens of medieval times. She didn't marry into her role as queen. Instead, she gained her crown by loving and giving birth to our Lord and King, Jesus Christ.

When we think about the meaning of "regal," it is hard to associate the term with a poor peasant girl. Think back to the opening lines of the Angelus in which Mary proclaims herself a simple handmaid of the Lord—a servant of the great king. And yet it is that attitude of service to God the Father and her deep love for her son that earn her a regal place in heaven.

Mary shows us the way to enter into the kingdom: love her son with all our heart and show that love by being a servant.

Meditation

When you think about a queen, what images come to mind? Now think about what you know about the life of the Virgin Mary. She shows us the way to enter into the royal kingdom of God. Consider how you can live more the way Mary did.

THE QUEEN REJOICES

Some popular Marian devotions focus on the sorrows Mary suffered in her lifetime. When Mary and Joseph took the infant Jesus to the Temple to consecrate him to God, Mary met Simeon, who prophesied about her forthcoming suffering, saying, "and you yourself a sword will pierce" (Lk 2:35). This is the first of the Seven Sorrows of Mary, a traditional Catholic devotion that focuses our meditation on the meaning of this prophecy.

When we reflect on the Easter joy of the Resurrection, we do not forget the sacrifices we made during Lent to get here. That suffering—even when it has not been too burdensome—makes the joy of Easter even more satisfying. After all, Easter candy tends to taste just a little bit better than usual to those who have abstained from sweets for forty days.

Imagine the great joy Mary felt at her son's Resurrection after her great sorrow in witnessing his suffering and death. This is the joy we call to mind in the Regina Caeli. We exhort Mary—who suffered so much pain—to rejoice again in her son's Resurrection. In proclaiming her joy, we ask her to share that joy with us as well. In memory of her sorrow, we rejoice that the Resurrection is here.

Meditation

If you are meditating on this prayer during the season of Easter, think back to your forty-day Lenten journey. What did you sacrifice or give up on the way to Christ's death on the Cross? How excited were you to have once again that which you gave up?

CLOUDS OF HEAVEN

To imagine heaven and not think of clouds is almost impossible. Classic and popular art and film have ingrained this imagery in our minds. Even the Bible mentions clouds when it describes Jesus' Ascension (Acts 1:9) and Second Coming (Mt 24:30; Rv 1:7).

Whether you enjoy flying or not, you have to admit that being in an airplane and flying above, through, and around the clouds is breathtakingly beautiful. It is hard to comprehend that what we're seeing is real—it's as if we're watching a movie outside the windows. It makes sense, then, to imagine that heaven will match and yet somehow exceed the beauty of the clouds in our skies.

We do not have to fly in planes to witness the beauty of this world. There is beauty everywhere if we take the time to stop and observe the world around us. This beauty of creation, properly appreciated, can inspire within us feelings of joy and gratitude and lead us to praise God. We may have to wait to experience the beauty of our heavenly home, but we don't have to wait to find joy in the beauty of our earthly home.

Meditation

Take some time today to observe the beauty of the world around you. Go outside and experience nature. Whether the sun is shining or the rain is pouring down, thank

God for the beauty around you. Through those acts of gratitude, you will open yourself up to experience the Resurrection joy we proclaim in the Regina Caeli.

FINALLY, WE CAN PROCLAIM ALLELUIA

As little girls, our daughters were always sticklers about Alleluias during Lent. When a Vacation Bible School CD would play in the car with a song that had an alleluia in it, my girls would shout to us to skip to the next song before it was too late. This is because during the Lenten liturgies, the Catholic Church does not say alleluia before the Gospel nor do we sing any songs with alleluia in it. We save it for Easter. I remember one Easter Mass when my two-year-old, who was paying more attention to the ribbon in the hymnal than to what was going on at the altar, suddenly stopped in amazement during the Gospel acclamation and, pointing to the choir, shouted up at me, "Alleluia, Daddy!"

There are many times in our lives when the alleluias are set aside for a little while. We may have a bad day or bad week. We may fall into a rut at work or in a relationship. We can find ourselves just going through the motions. Yet these dips in life, these moments of dryness, will someday come to an end. At some point, we will again hear and feel that alleluia. It may require patience.

It may seem as though that time will never come, but it will. Like the surprise my daughter felt when she heard alleluia again at Mass for the first time in forty days, we, too, will find joy in life again.

Meditation

Are there any areas in your life that feel empty and unexciting? Are you in a rut of some sort? Offer these parts of your life to God as you pray the Regina Caeli. Ask for the Queen of Heaven's intercession that God give you back that spirit of alleluia once again.

For He, Whom You Did Merit to Bear, Alleluia

BECOMING A CHRIST BEARER

Of the many titles of Mary we proclaim in the Angelus and Regina Caeli, one of the most subtle is "Christ bearer." As the Mother of Christ, who is God, Mary became the Mother of God. She carried our God in her womb. She brought him along on a journey to visit her cousin Elizabeth. She bore him on the trip to Bethlehem and there gave birth to him. It didn't stop at his birth, though. She brought him with her to many other places during his childhood. Then, after he had died, risen, and ascended into heaven, she continued to bear her son in the world by the power of the Holy Spirit. She, too, was present at Pentecost. Like the Apostles, she carried forth the Spirit of Christ in the world.

Like Mary, we can bear Christ within the world. We can take him with us into everything we do in our days. We can merit our bearing of him by our humble service and ceaseless consideration of God's will in our lives. Then, through this commitment to become Christ bearers, we can rejoice with Mary and find the alleluias in our lives.

Meditation

Are there any areas in your life where you find it difficult to bring Christ with you? Such areas may be where we need God the most. They can become the greatest opportunities for transformation. Find the alleluias in your life by imagining Christ with you throughout every part of this day—at work, at home, while hanging out with friends, even in the simple and mundane activities of your day.

THE MERITS OF MARY

When Boy or Girl Scouts accomplish certain goals, they earn merit badges. The badges are sewn onto vests displaying every badge they have earned. These accomplishments become a part of their identity as scouts.

An interesting analogy can be made here about our spiritual merit as it relates to God and our salvation. No one has any merit at all apart from God. God is like the vest. Any merit we may have is linked to our relationship with him. Just as the merit badge is sewn onto the vest, our merit is linked to God.

God's infinite love for us far outweighs any action we could possibly take to merit that love from him. He bestows his grace on us despite our faults. That grace— God's sharing of his life with us—enables us to experience his love and extend that love to others. God's grace, in other words, is the source of any merit we could possess. Without that link to God, the merit is as meaningless as an unattached merit badge that is lost or tucked away in a drawer somewhere.

In the Regina Caeli, we address Mary as the one who "did merit to bear" Jesus Christ. Is there any better description of spiritual merit than this? Overcome by the power of the Holy Spirit, Mary became the Mother of God. Because of her faith and fullness of grace, she did merit to bear the Son of God to the world.

Maybe merit comes down not so much to what we can do through our own hard work, but to what God can do through us. Mary, therefore, merited to bear Jesus because she allowed God to work through her. We venerate her because of God's great work in and through her.

Meditation

Reflect on your own merit as a future Christian saint. Don't think of all your hard work to be holy or your extra efforts to pray and do good works. Think instead of the great gift of God's grace in your life. How have you been touched by his love? How has he been with you, guiding and sustaining you in your daily life?

PUTTING THE ANGELUS IN PERSPECTIVE

If the two prayers weren't linked by long tradition, you could easily miss the connection between our Easter Regina Caeli and the Angelus. There is good reason for the pairing. The Regina Caeli in many ways puts our Angelus meditation on the Annunciation and Incarnation into perspective. The Annunciation isn't complete without the Resurrection.

Mary, the Queen of Heaven, is the Mother of God. Her merit is due to her deeply intimate relationship with God. She is God's mother. It sounds almost blasphemous to say, but it is true. Mary is the Mother of God—of the One who is risen from the dead, the One who conquered death itself. The Resurrection only happened because a lowly handmaid said yes to an angel announcing the virgin birth of a son.

We don't think about Christmas very often during the season of Easter. Maybe we should. The seasons of Advent and Christmas—seasons to remember the preparation for and event of the birth of Christ—find completion in the season of Easter—a season to celebrate the Resurrection of Christ and our new birth. In the same way, the Angelus finds completion in the Regina Caeli.

Meditation

As you pray the Regina Caeli today, remember the Annunciation and the birth of Christ. Those stories find their fulfillment in the joys of the Easter Resurrection. How do they take on new meaning in the context of the Resurrection?

NO HAIL MARYS

The contrast between praying the Angelus and praying the Regina Caeli is probably felt most clearly in the lack of the triple Hail Marys that have been at the core of the Angelus practice for centuries. In the Regina Caeli, we repeat other words much more fitting for the season of Easter.

We repeat the word "alleluia" six times and the word "joy" four times, five if you translate the Latin word *gaude* as "be joyful" instead of "be glad." Alleluia is a word that expresses our praise to God. It isn't something we say simply because we like God a lot or think he is really great. We praise God with our alleluias because of his great work: he has risen from the dead and saved us from our sins. The Resurrection can make us joyful. Out of that joy, we give praise to God.

While you may miss the prayerful reminders of the Incarnation in the Hail Marys, our frequent repetition of "alleluia" and "rejoice" in the Regina Caeli during this

Easter season enables us to praise God in a different way. Not only has he come into the world and dwelt among us, he has died just as we will die and gone on to conquer death. This is certainly something to praise him for.

Meditation

Since you won't pray the Hail Mary during your Easter season Regina Caeli, take some time today to pray for Mary's intercession with the joy of the Resurrection in your heart. Keep in your mind and heart the emotions that meditating on Jesus' Resurrection can bring you. Remember, it was only through Mary's yes that God's plan of salvation came into the world through the Resurrection of his Son.

Has Risen,
as He Said, Alleluia

HE SAID HE WOULD RISE

Look closely at the gospel stories of Christ's Resurrection. The response of his disciples is very consistent. When they hear of the empty tomb, they respond in disbelief. When John arrives at the tomb, it takes seeing the burial cloths there to help him realize that what Jesus foretold has come true: he has risen from the dead. Before seeing the empty tomb with his own eyes, John's gospel tells us, John did not understand. Now, having seen, he believes (see Jn 20:2–9).

Thomas the Apostle has a similar experience. He misses Jesus' first appearance to the disciples and will not believe the others' testimony about his rising. He has to see Jesus himself to believe. Jesus says to him, and indirectly to us, that those who believe without having the opportunity to see him directly with their own eyes are blessed (see Jn 20:24–29).

Have you ever considered our belief in the Resurrection? We weren't there to see the Risen Lord. We can, however, place our trust in the testimony of the Apostles that has been passed down to us through scripture and tradition.

The other way to have faith in the Resurrection is to find the joy of God's presence at work in your life today. We may not be able to see God, but we can certainly see his work in the world if we are willing to let down our guard and trust that what he says is true.

Meditation

Think about your own belief in the Resurrection for a moment. Where does your belief in the Resurrection find its foundation?

Pray for Us to God, Alleluia

A PRAYING QUEEN

Let's compare for a moment the intercession we ask of Mary in the Angelus and the requests we place before her in the Regina Caeli. In the Angelus, we ask the Mother of God to pray that "we may be made worthy of the promises of Christ." In the Regina Caeli we are not as specific. After we ask Mary to rejoice early in the prayer, we ask her to pray for us. What would the joyful Mary ask for on our behalf? Undoubtedly that we will experience the same joy she has in heaven.

Later in the Regina Caeli, when we make our petition to God, we remind him of what we asked Mary to intercede for: that "we may obtain the joys of everlasting life." We may be blessed with joy in our lives today, but we also look ahead to the joys of our life with the Lord in heaven. This petition to God is not very different from the prayer request we set before Mary in the Angelus ("that we may be made worth of the promises of Christ"). Jesus promises us eternal joy in heaven even if we can never fully realize it in this life.

What a comfort this is! If we pray the Angelus and Regina Caeli on a daily basis, that means that Mary is asking her Son to grant us the joy in heaven each and every day. How exciting! With great expectation we can look forward to our future union with God and to the joy beyond all earthly joys.

Meditation

Take a moment and feel comforted. Mary, the Mother of God, is praying for your joy today. She is there before God in heaven praying on your behalf. She wants you to experience the same joy that she experiences as Queen of Heaven. How could he turn down his mother? That joy is coming. Get ready.

Rejoice and Be Glad, O Virgin Mary, Alleluia

CULTIVATING GLADNESS

Think for a moment about the ways in which you have used the word "glad." We often say something like "I am glad *x*, *y*, and *z* happened." Or we might use the word in response to someone else's news, as in "Oh, I'm so glad to hear that."

Gladness is an emotion almost always expressed as a response. Something good happens, and we feel glad. It is slightly different from rejoicing because rejoicing requires an active posture. In the original Latin of the Regina Caeli, "be glad" is the translation of *gaude* while *gaudete* is translated as "rejoice." To rejoice is to do something active, while gladness is a state of being.

Why make the distinction? It is because we often choose, in response to certain events, not to be glad. Something happens in the world or to us, and we choose not to see the good in it. When we take some time to react to the events in our lives with gratitude, we can cultivate a state of gladness.

Meditation

Spend some time today reflecting on everything that happened to you so far today. Offer gratitude to the Lord for these events. Choose to be glad even if you didn't think the day was as good as it could have been.

THE VIRGIN MARY

With the invocation of Mary as virgin we recall in a small way the Angelus. Christ was conceived in Mary by the power of the Holy Spirit. According to Catholic Church teaching, Mary remained a virgin her entire life. Often, when we talk about Mary's virginity, we think of her purity—not purity in a rudimentary, she-never-had-sex sense, but purity in the sense of holiness before God. Mary was and is the supreme example of human holiness.

As we reflect on the Resurrection today while we pray the Regina Caeli, let us consider the ways in which God is calling us to be more holy. He continually calls us to be holy. He does not shame us for the unholy things we've done. Purity is a gift that he offers continuously. We have reason to rejoice and be glad because, just like the Virgin Mary, we are made holy by being filled with God's grace.

Meditation

In which areas of your life has God made you holy? Instead of thinking of where you fall short, give thanks for the ways in which you have been made holy by the grace of God. In which situations or relationships in your life are you able to love with a self-giving love? In what ways are you already living out God's will?

For the Lord
Has Truly Risen, Alleluia

TRULY RISEN

Sometimes we have to say it to believe it: Jesus Christ died, but then he rose again. He died, but he came back to life. Like many things we profess as Christians, this belief can be easy to take for granted. We have heard about Jesus' rising so frequently in our lifetimes that we lose our sense of the outlandishness of the Resurrection. Jesus' coming back to life is highly unlikely and unbelievable. Even the apostles could not believe it for themselves.

In the Regina Caeli, we confirm our belief in the Resurrection two times, as if we are reassuring ourselves: yes, "the Lord has truly risen." As members of the Church community, we proclaim together Christ's rising from the dead. We have reason to join with Mary in rejoicing beyond belief that Christ is risen.

If we look closely at our Christian beliefs, not to doubt them but to appreciate them as gifts, they can be sources of great joy because behind every belief is a revelation of God's love for us. The Resurrection is proof of God's incredible love for us. He gives us the gift of new life. He gave us this gift through great suffering and death.

We have every reason to frequently proclaim "alleluia" in response.

Meditation

Think back to Lent and Holy Week: through his suffering, death, and Resurrection, Christ shows us God's infinite love and brings us incredible joy. With your Regina Caeli today, express gratitude to God for the gift of the Resurrection.

O God, Who Gave Joy to the World through the Resurrection of Thy Son, Our Lord Jesus Christ, Grant, We Beseech Thee

THE SOURCE OF JOY

We cannot force ourselves to feel joy. We can act as though we're happy and put a smile on our faces. Sometimes this can even give us a feeling of happiness. Joy, though, is different. It has to come from somewhere. Its source is outside—or deep inside—of us. We can search for and accept it, but we cannot fake it.

Joy is a gift from God that God gives us in many different ways. We can experience joy among family and friends, realizing how much we are loved by them and blessed by God. We can experience joy when encountering beauty in creation and we can experience joy in response to certain events.

The joy we proclaim in the Regina Caeli has its source in the Resurrection. God "gave joy to the world through the Resurrection." Even without the Resurrection, we would certainly have a lot to be thankful for:

God created us. He chose a special people to be his, and we are part of that people. He even became one of us to show us the path to joyful living. Ultimately, though, it is the Resurrection that is our true source of joy. Through the Resurrection, we can finally be fully united with the Lord and with his people. This is something that inspires true joy within us.

Meditation

Imagine, for a moment, the joys of heaven: the experience of the Lord's perfect love and reunion with our lost loved ones. If you can, let the joy of the anticipation of heaven well up inside of you. Search for it. At the very least, give thanks to Jesus for the gift of new life through the Resurrection.

JOY TO THE WORLD

The hymn "Joy to the World" is traditionally, of course, a Christmas carol. We don't often think of it during the season of Easter, but it certainly expresses the same sentiment as the Regina Caeli. Just as we repeated the sounding joy of Jesus' birth, so, too, can we proclaim joy to the world during this season of Easter. God gave joy to the world through the Resurrection of Christ.

The words of the song are based on Psalm 98, which encourages the reader to sing praise and shout with joy to the Lord. If you read this psalm closely, you can't help but think of the Resurrection with every verse. The words sing of marvelous deeds, victory, all the ends of the earth, rivers, mountains, justice, fairness, and governance—all of which take on new meaning in light of the Resurrection.

As we continue to pray this wonderful prayer and meditate on the meaning of the Resurrection, let us take moments throughout our day to appreciate what God has done. Let us not stop at speaking our thanks to God; let us give him the full song of praise that he really deserves.

Meditation

Pick your favorite verse from the Christmas carol "Joy to the World." Sing it in your head, but think of the Resurrection instead of the birth of Christ. Make the words of the song your words as you praise God for the gift of the Resurrection.

That through the Intercession of the Virgin Mary, His Mother

INTERCESSORY PRAYER

Will you pray for me? I mean it. Please, say a prayer for the author of this book. I would really appreciate it. To be able to pray to God on behalf of someone is an incredible gift and an amazing responsibility.

Each time we pray the Regina Caeli we ask that Mary pray for us. Why? What do we hope her prayers will do for us? We hope to experience the joys of everlasting life. These are the same joys that Mary herself is experiencing right now. She doesn't share that joy with us directly but asks God to bestow it upon us. We are united in joy through intercessory prayer.

Back to my prayer request. When you pray for me and I pray for you—and I am praying for you as I write this—we are united together. That same joy of everlasting life is made manifest through our mutual concern for one another. When I know someone is praying for me, it gives me hope. It makes me smile. I experience a sense of joy.

Thank you for your prayers.

Meditation

Ask someone to pray for you today. We are not afraid to ask Mary to pray for us each time we pray the Regina Caeli. Let's keep going. Ask a friend or family member to pray for you and promise to pray for them in return. Those prayers unite you together in love and hope for the joy of everlasting life.

MARY, MOTHER OF MERCY

In the Hail Holy Queen, another Catholic prayer highlighting the royalty of Mary, we call her the "Mother of Mercy." I love that title. Mary is the Mother of Jesus, in whom we find infinite mercy. She is, therefore, the Mother of Mercy. Our shame and guilt are healed through the mercy of God. In him we find love, unity, and hope for our future.

Mary, who is full of grace, is also full of mercy. She intercedes for us not only because we ask but because of her overwhelming desire to be merciful. Inspired by her relationship with her son, she pours out her prayers on our behalf. She wants us to know the same mercy she knows so well as the Mother of God.

This is what mercy compels us to do: filled with the joy of God's mercy, we go out and extend mercy to others. We help and listen and serve wherever we are needed. Through that mercy, others come to know Christ in deeper ways, too, and get to experience mercy directly from him themselves.

Meditation

When you ask the Holy Queen, Mother of Mercy, to pray for you today, focus in a special way on God's merciful, healing love. Ask that his mercy to be extended to you and to anyone you know who in a particular way needs that mercy today. If you can, be a vessel of that mercy by reaching out to that person.

We May Obtain the Joys of Everlasting Life

HAVING MORE HOPE

Is our anticipation of the joys of everlasting life limited? Are we truly able to grasp the depth of joy that heaven will provide? People always say that you can't really know what heaven will be like, but they can list for you metaphors, feelings, and thoughts about what God has in store for us—things that they hope for.

As Christians, we believe that the joy of everlasting life is truly beyond measure. It is a mystery to be unfolded before us. Quite possibly, our hope and anticipation are too small. We often associate heaven with images of clouds, golden gates, trumpets, angels, and people walking around in white garments. While these images can be helpful, they are too small. We need to have hope in something much, much greater. Praying the Regina Caeli each day can help us broaden our horizon of hope in the joys of everlasting life.

Meditation

Think of the most joyful moment of your life. Now imagine an even more joyful experience. Can you do it? Pretty difficult, huh? Recognizing that the joys of everlasting life are far beyond our comprehension, let us turn to God in hope and gratitude for the amazing gift he has in store for us.

FEEL THE FLOW

The "flow state" is a concept coined by psychologist Mihaly Csikszentmihalyi in his research and in his book, *Flow.* Athletes call it "being in the zone." You experience it when you are so engaged in an activity that time seems to stand still; your consciousness seems to exist almost outside of time. Many people who experience this flow state begin to crave it. They try desperately to recreate it at every possible opportunity. Why? Because the experience of flow is the experience of joy.

Joy is not happiness. Joy comes with the feeling of peacefulness that is present also in the flow state. When we are in the zone, we connect with our true selves. We are doing the work that we love and able to act without any consciousness of the world around us. It is easy to question ourselves and doubt our abilities. We struggle to achieve some goal or carry out some task, and the frustration takes a physical toll on us. When we are in a flow state, though, we are at peace—a peace that feels like joy.

I have a hunch that the joys of everlasting life will be a lot like flow. Just as people report feeling as though they were outside of time while in the zone, so too will we be outside of time in heaven. Our everlasting life won't feel long at all; instead, we will feel like we're in the zone without being bogged down by time.

Meditation

Have you ever experienced the flow state? What was that experience like? Would you call it joy? How do you think that experience might compare to the joys of everlasting life?

THE JOY OF A SAINT

Have you ever wondered if heaven might get boring? For something to be everlasting means it will never end. Sure, we will have everything we could possibly want. The people we love will be there. Things will be amazing—never better. Yet, the idea of doing the same thing for "everlasting" time can be difficult to understand as joyful.

This is because seeking something different is our default perspective. We pursue things that are different and better. This affinity for growth keeps us interested, engaged, motivated, and excited. We look for better jobs, better homes, better cars, better stuff, and an all-around better way of life. But if we always strive for the better, and if in heaven there is nothing "better," how can we be happy?

As Christians, we place our hope in God, trusting that one day we will be united with him and all his children in everlasting life. I do not know what everlasting life will be like, but I do know that we will be filled with the joys of everlasting life and we won't be bored. I suspect that joy is possible in eternity only insofar as we are able to be satisfied with what we have on earth rather than constantly seeking something better.

Regardless of what heaven is like, we do know what we will be like. We will be saints and we will be filled with everlasting joy. We will be people so devoid of selfishness that our only desires will be to be with God, to please God, and to share his love with others. That's joy—the joy of a saint.

I daresay that we don't have to be in heaven to experience this joy. If we truly want to prepare for the joys of everlasting life, it is time to start living like a saint now. Instead of constantly pursuing the "better," let us be joyful with and grateful for what we have.

Meditation

Examine your personal desires for something better than what you have. Have you convinced yourself that you can experience joy only after fulfilling that desire? As you pray today, consider how you might find joy regardless of what you have: the job, house, stuff, and people in your life. Experiencing the joy of everlasting life doesn't have to wait until after death. We can start to experience it right now if we are open to it as a gift from Christ our Lord.

Notes

1. Benedict XVI, "On the Word of God in the Life and Mission of the Church," Apostolic Exhortation *Verbum Domini* (Vatican City: Libreria Editrice Vaticana, 2010), 88, http://w2.vatican.va/content/benedict-xvi/en/apost_exhortations/documents/hf_ben-xvi_exh_20100930_verbum-domini.html.

2. Irenaeus, *Against Heresies*, Book III, 22:4.

3. John Donne, "Meditation XVII," *Devotions upon Emergent Occasions*, http://www.online-literature.com/donne/409/.

4. Napoleon Hill, *Think and Grow Rich: The Landmark Bestseller—Now Revised and Updated for the 21st Century* (New York: Jeremy P. Tarcher/Penguin, 2005), 51.

5. Lewis Hyde, *The Gift: Creativity and the Artist in the Modern World* (New York: Vintage Books, 2007), xvi.

6. Irenaeus, *Against Heresies*, Book III, 22:4.

7. Francis, Twitter post, June 3, 2013, 3:05 a.m., https://twitter.com/Pontifex.

8. John Paul II, Angelus address, March 4, 1979 (Vatican City: Libreria Editrice Vaticana, 1979), 1, https://w2.vatican.va/content/john-paul-ii/en/angelus/1979/documents/hf_jp-ii_ang_19790304.html.

9. *The Usual Suspects*, directed by Bryan Singer (1995; Beverly Hills, CA: MGM Studios).

10. C. S. Lewis, *The Screwtape Letters* (San Francisco: HarperOne, 2001), xx.

JARED DEES is the creator of the popular website *The Religion Teacher*, a site that provides practical resources and effective teaching strategies to religious educators. A respected graduate of the Alliance for Catholic Education program at the University of Notre Dame, Dees earned master's degrees in education and theology, both from Notre Dame. He has volunteered for and worked in a wide variety of Catholic ministries, including Catholic schools, parish religious education, youth ministry, campus ministry, RCIA, and adult faith formation. Dees is the digital marketing manager at Ave Maria Press and the author of *31 Days to Becoming a Better Religious Educator*, and *To Heal, Proclaim, and Teach*. His articles have appeared in *Momentum*, *CATECHIST*, *Catechetical Leader*, and on numerous websites. Dees lives in South Bend, Indiana, with his wife and four children.